HOW TO
DRAW
GRAFFITI
ART

LEARN TO MASTER TAGS, WILDSTYLE, URBAN LETTERING AND CREATIVE PIECING

How to Draw Graffiti Art will introduce you to a wide arrange of styles, including an emphasis on wild style and urban lettering also known as bubble lettering, that will enhance your skills and creativity when creating tags.

Each tag will include a description of the graffiti word used as each word has a unique meaning to welcome you into the graffiti world.

Legal Notice:

This book is copyright protected. This book is only for personal use. You cannot amend, distribute, sell, use, quote or paraphrase any part, or the content within this book, without the consent of the author or publisher.

Disclaimer Notice:

Please note the information contained within this document is for educational and entertainment purposes only. All effort has been executed to present accurate, up to date, and reliable, complete information. No warranties of any kind are declared or implied. Readers acknowledge that the author is not engaging in the rendering of legal, financial, medical or professional advice. The content within this book has been derived from various sources. Please consult a licensed professional before attempting any techniques outlined in this book.

By reading this document, the reader agrees that under no circumstances is the author responsible for any losses, direct or indirect, which are incurred as a result of the use of information contained within this document, including, but not limited to, — errors, omissions, or inaccuracies.

Table of Contents

How to Draw Tags

Angels:

Graffiti art came to life due to well-known artists that made their mark and are respected in the community, angels are referred to the artists who have passed. Solute to the great!

how to DRAW a GRUNGE TAG

STEP 1

Draw the word ANGELS with simple letters. In this case we will make the letters somewhat separated

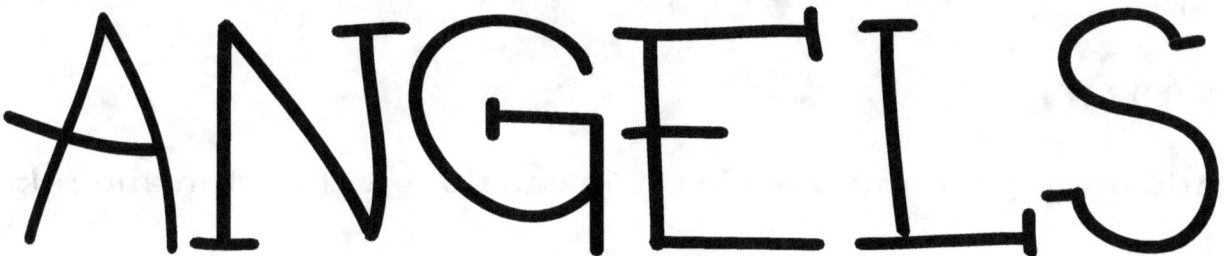

STEP 2

Add some serifs in this sketch and details

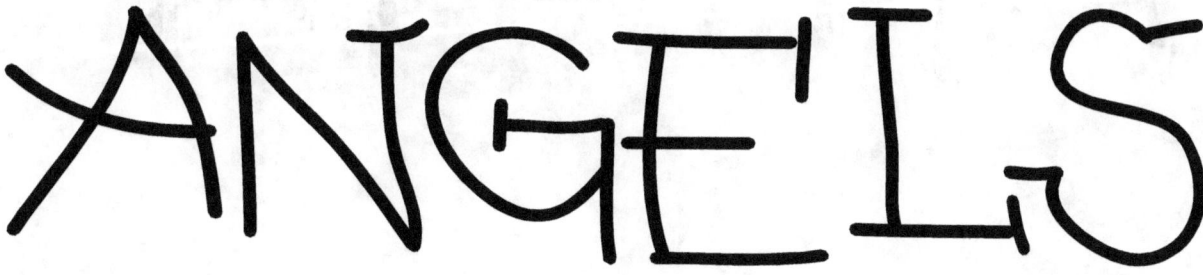

STEP 3

Customize sketch with more Floyd

STEP 4

Make some interesting lines that simulate wings at the extremes of the tag

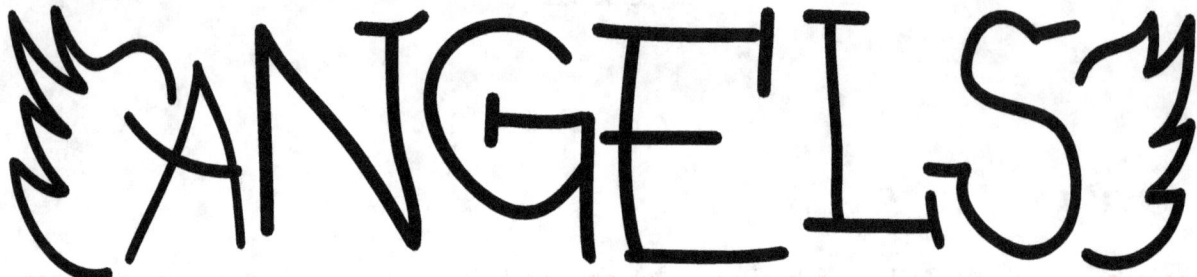

STEP 5

Now is the time to add some "drops" going down, with curved lines and points in a fine stroke

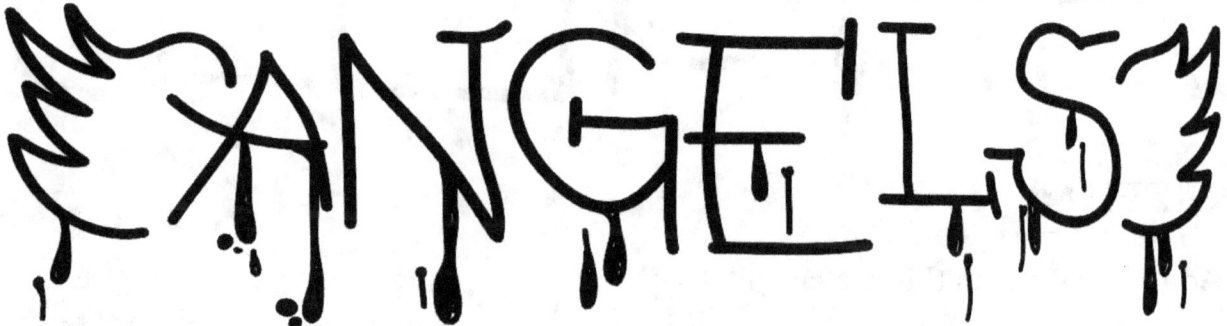

STEP 6

Add a spray around this idea. You can do it with cotton and ink.

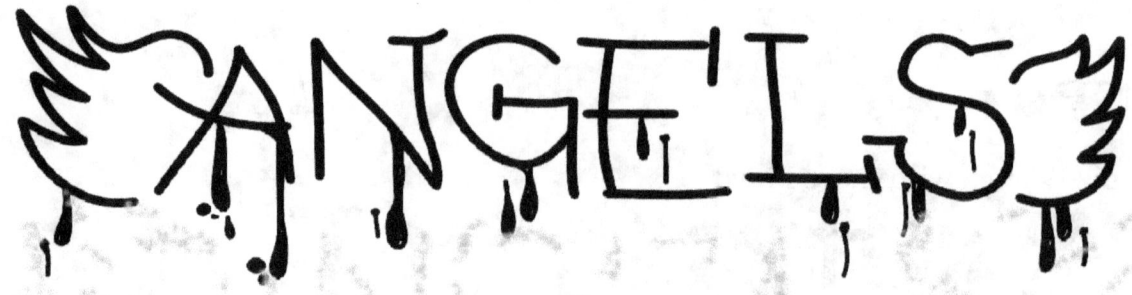

Bite:

Some art is too good to not duplicate! Bite is referred to a seasoned artist's ideas, lettering, color scheme and/or sometimes name being used by other artists!

how to DRAW a BROADWAY TAG

STEP 1

Draw the word BITE with simple letters. In this case we will make them very elongated and together

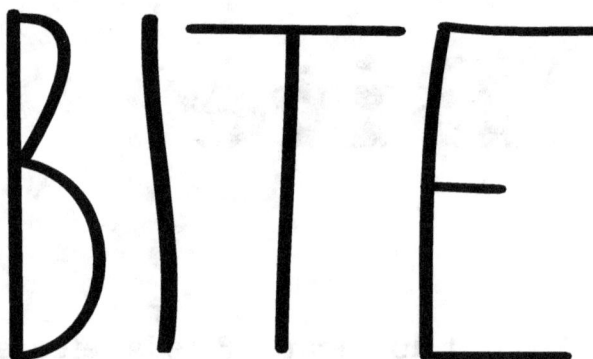

STEP 2

We will treat each letter separately. The curves of the B we will make angular. The I will include two diagonal serifs. We are going to lower the transverse line of the T a bit and make it at an angle. To E we will put two serifs at the end of each horizontal line and the middle line of the E will be done at the same angle as the transverse line of the T.

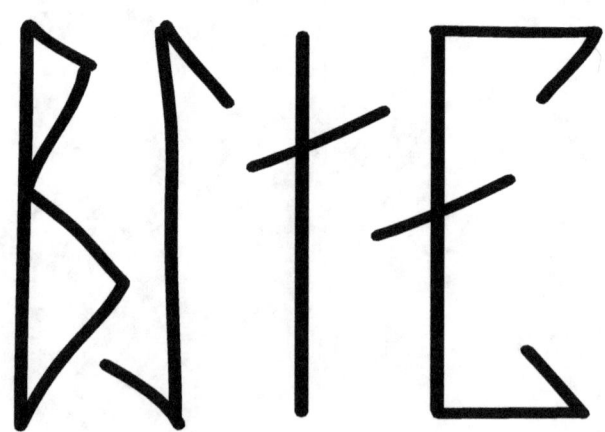

STEP 3

Connect the serifs with elongated discontinued lines

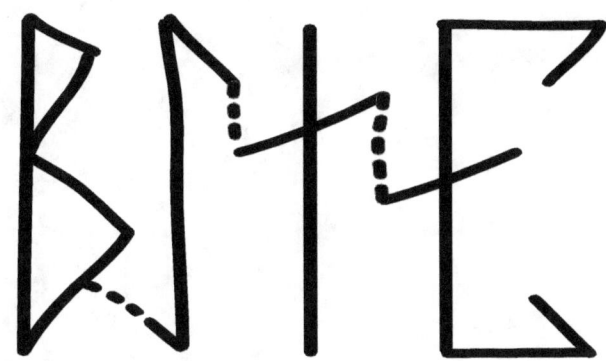

STEP 4

Add in extensions to some letters of this tag

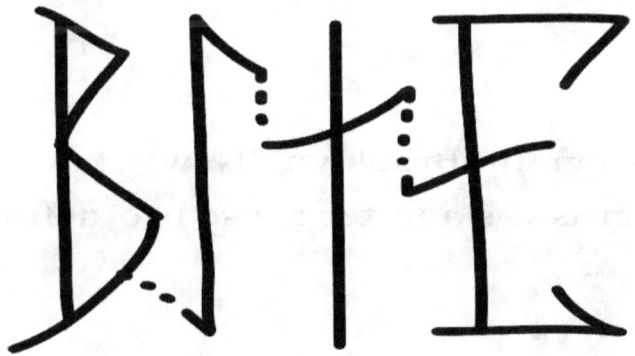

STEP 5

Draw a discontinuous 3D shadow with a fine stroke

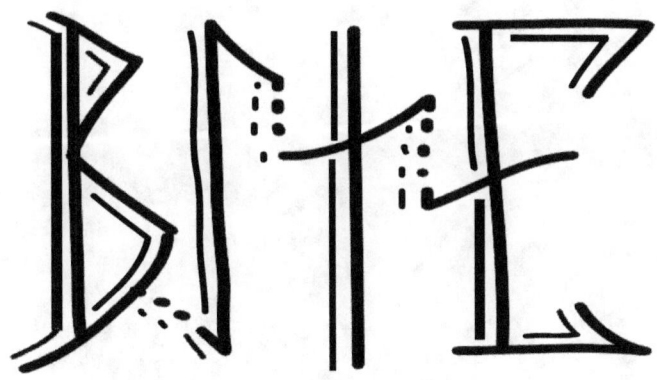

Cannon:

With an origination in Brooklyn, New York. Shout out to Brooklyn! Cannon is a slang term used to define spray paint cans

how to DRAW a OUTLINE TAG

STEP 1

Draw the word CANNON with simple letters. In this case we will make the letters tall

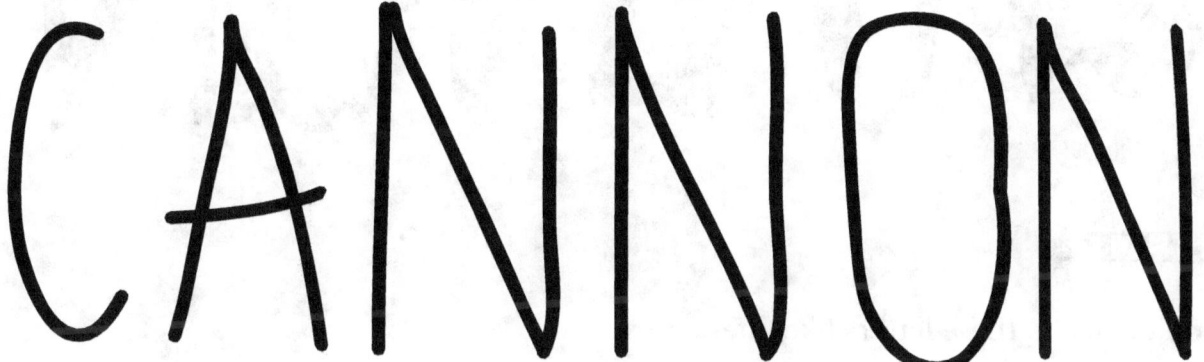

STEP 2

Next, add serifs at the end of some lines

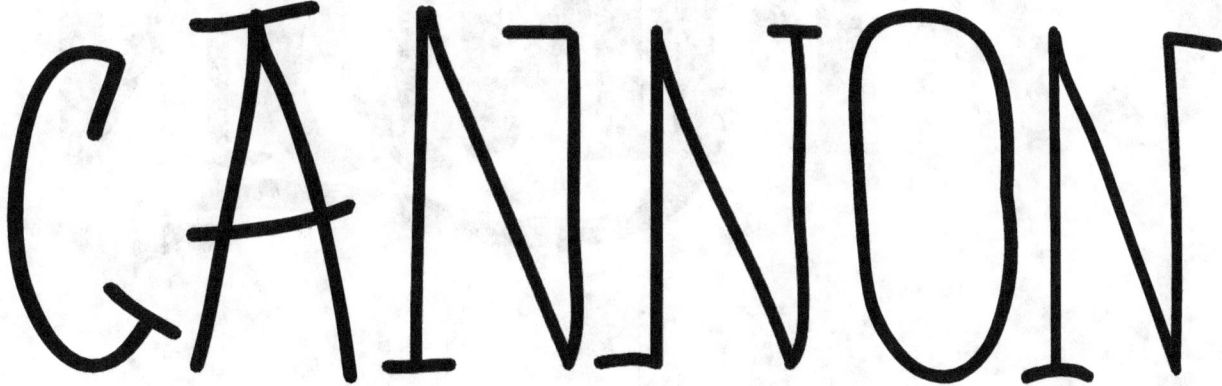

STEP 3

Draw the tag again bringing the letters closer together. Make the strokes from thin to thick

CANNON

STEP 4

Add details to these letters like lines or arrows

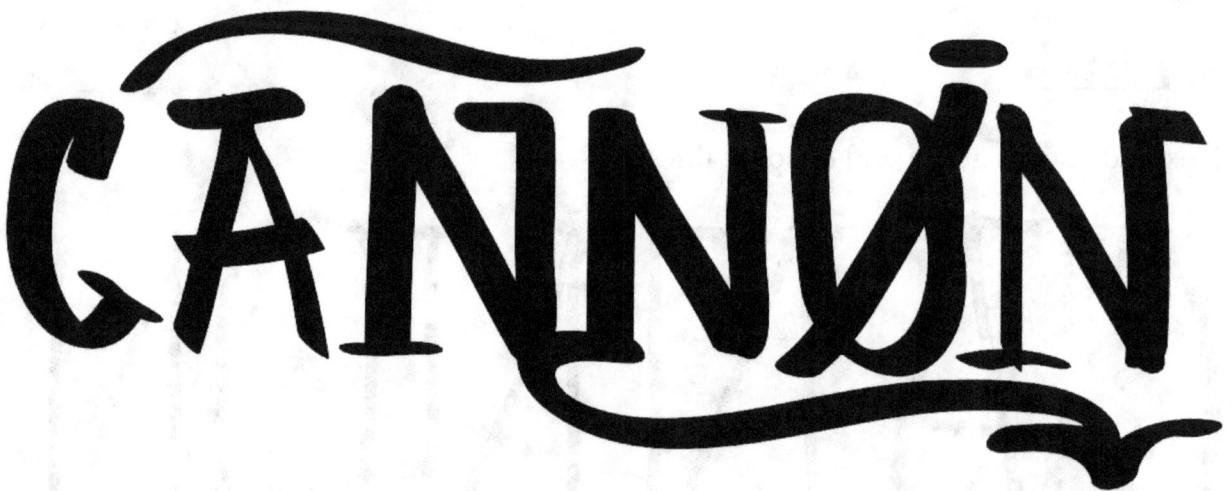

STEP 5

Use this as a template and draw an outline following the previous with a fine stroke

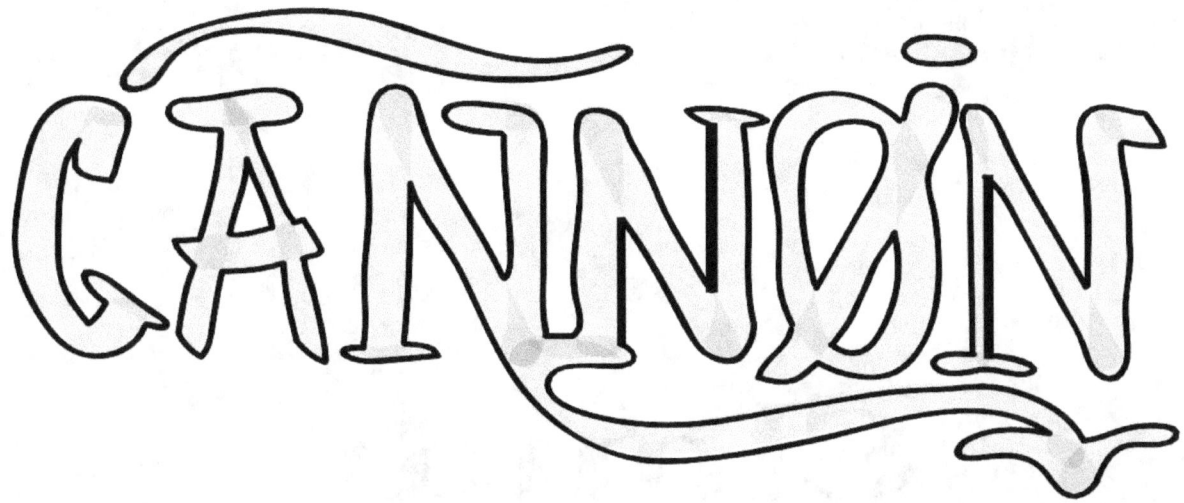

STEP 6

Shade a 3D effect in this tag with a fine line in the middle within each part of this area

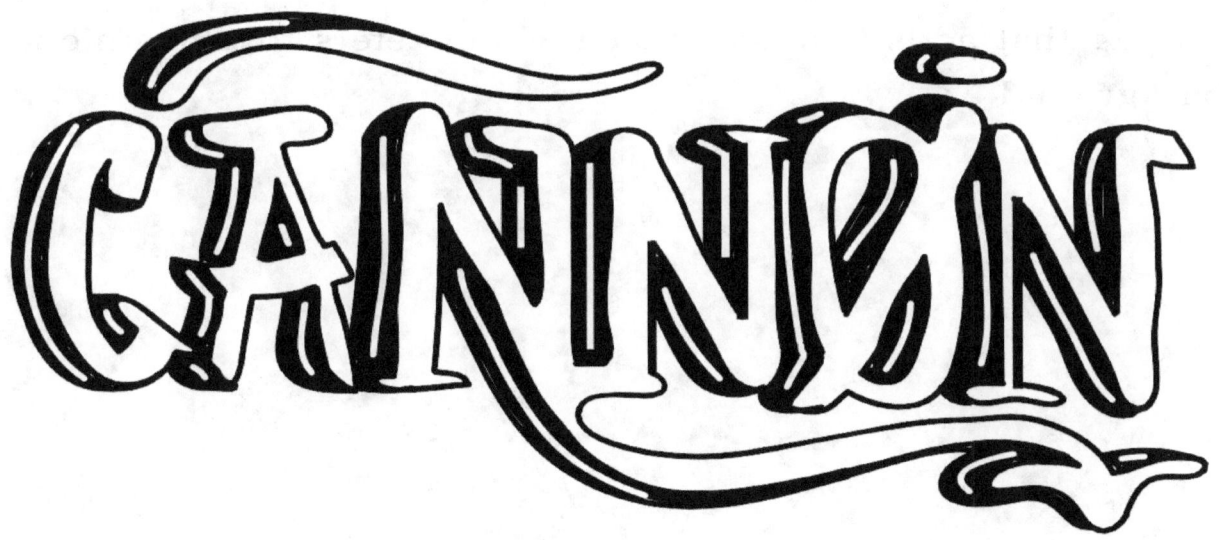

Cloud:

To a wide variety of tags there is a background that accompanies the tag that adds flair to a piece, cloud refers to that unique background

how to DRAW a TAG WITH An ORIENTATION

STEP 1

Draw two curved lines as the basis for the word

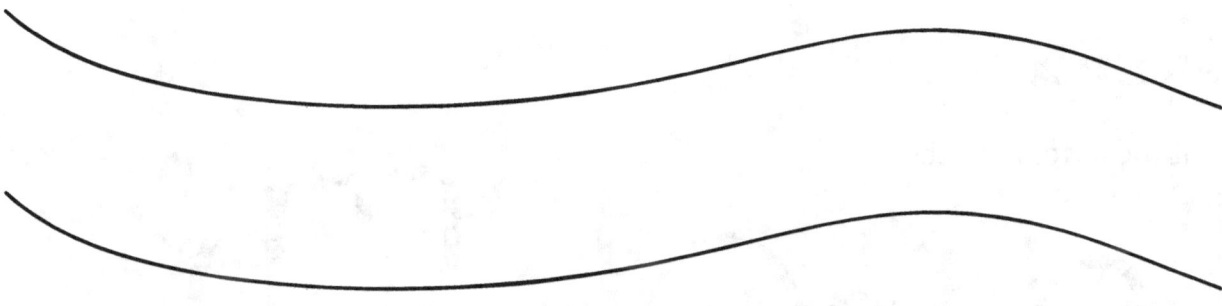

STEP 2

Draw the word CLOUD in simple letters following the template generated

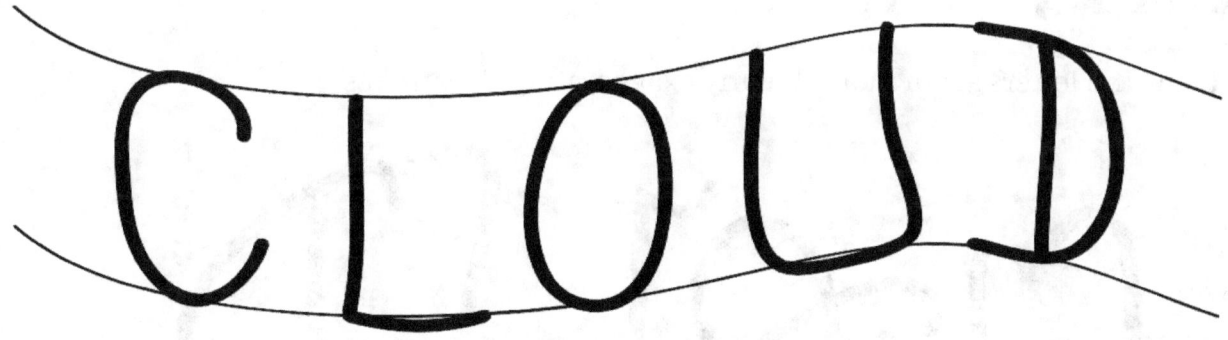

STEP 3

Erase the template lines and add in serifs to the letters

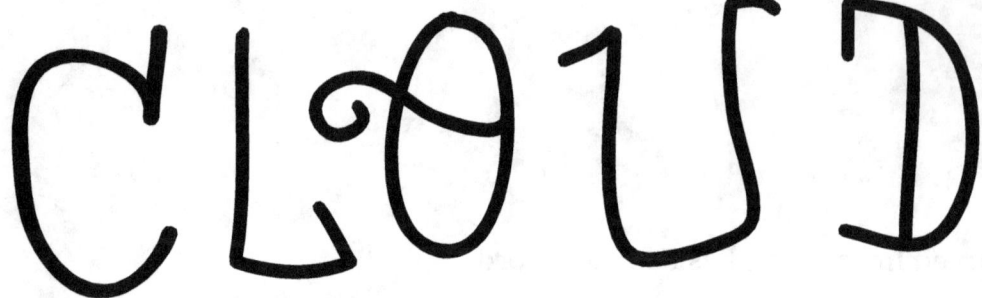

STEP 4

Put the letters together

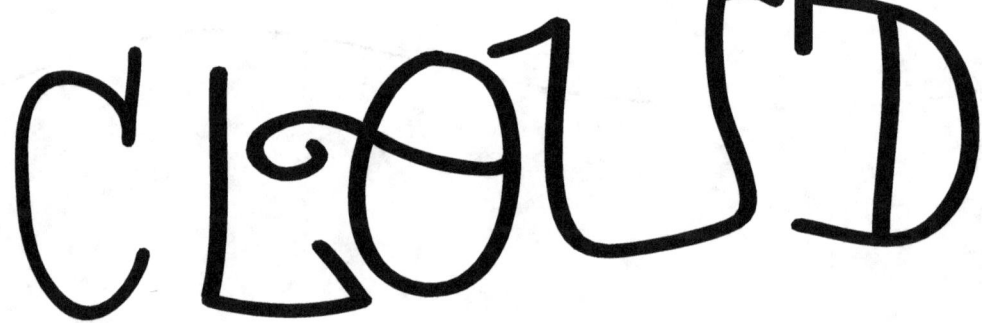

STEP 5

Draw the letters again more fluently exaggerating the strokes

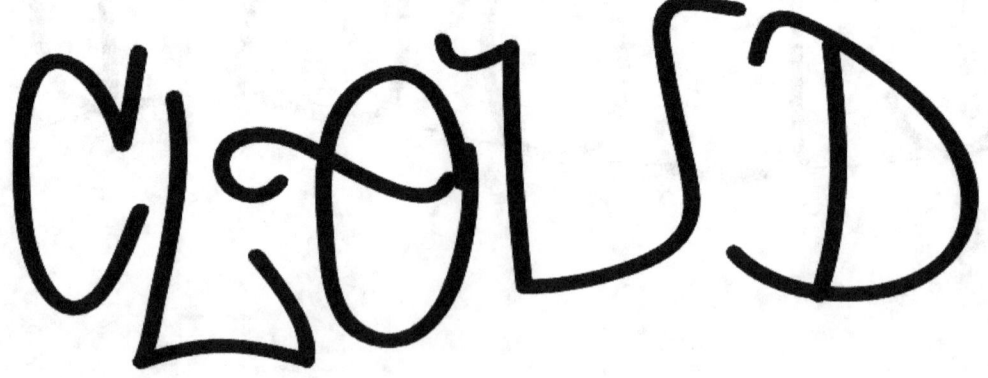

STEP 6

Add extra details like arrows to the letters

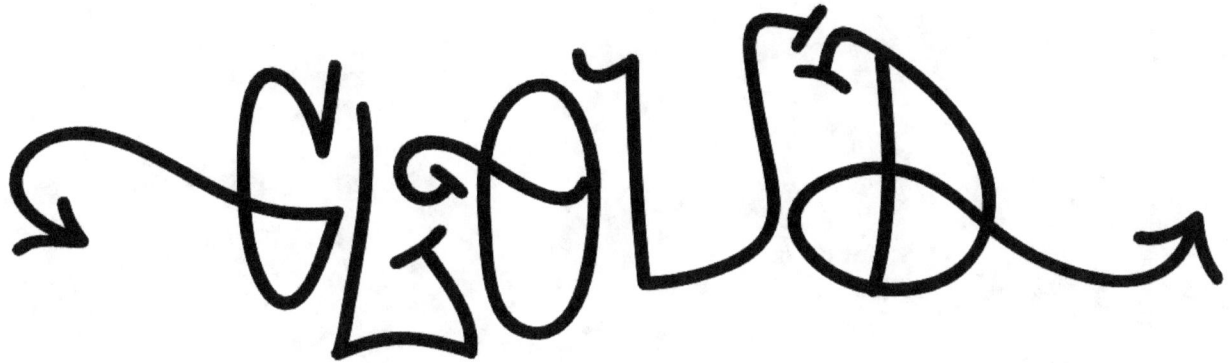

STEP 7

Add a cloud around the tag with a fine stroke

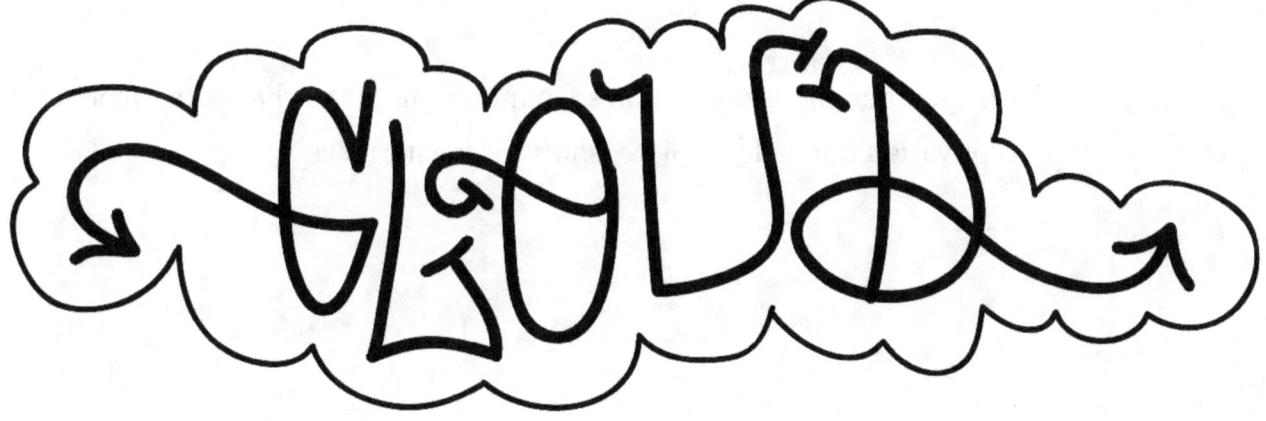

Pieces:

There are stylistic qualities that separate tags from one another, when a tag reaches a certain level of captivation it is called a piece, short for masterpiece

how to DRAW a SIMPLE TAG

STEP 1

Draw the word PIECES

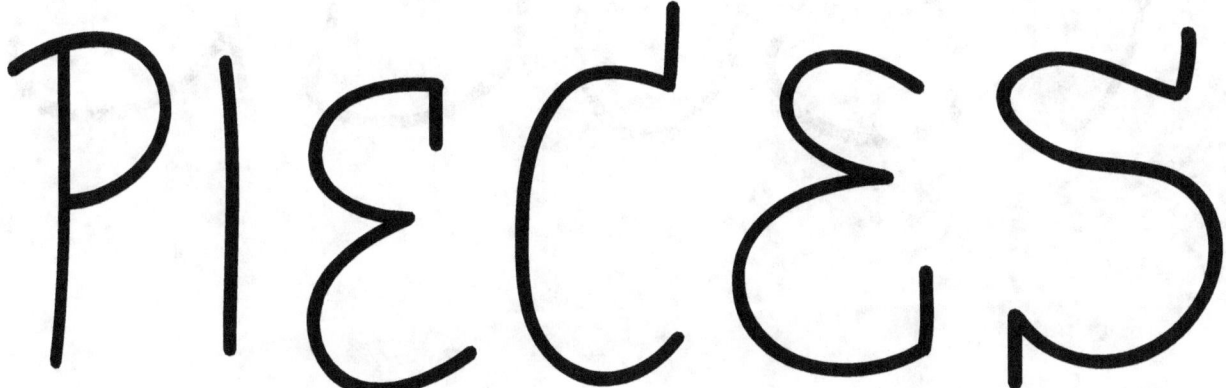

STEP 2

Add in serifs to some letters

STEP 3

Redraw the tag. Add an oval at the end of the I (halo). Curve the letters a bit

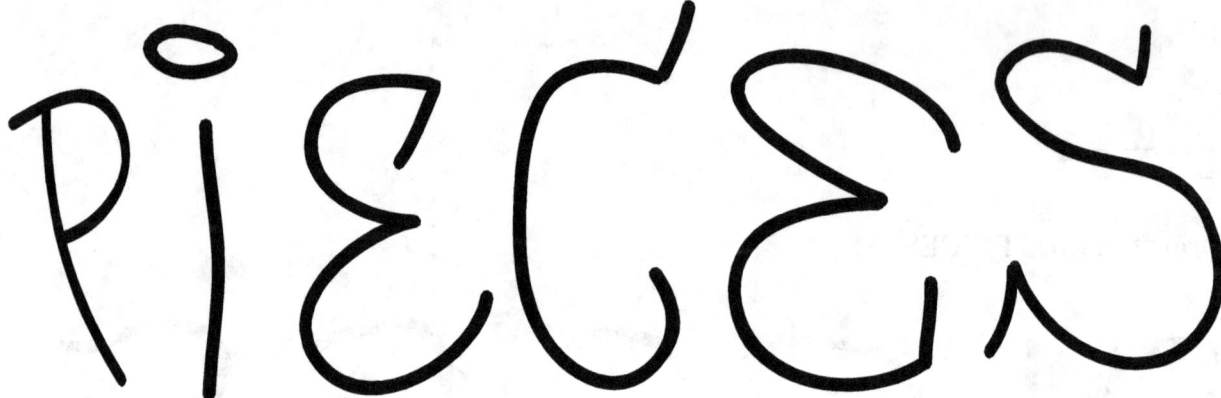

STEP 4

Draw the letters quickly and try to exaggerate the lines

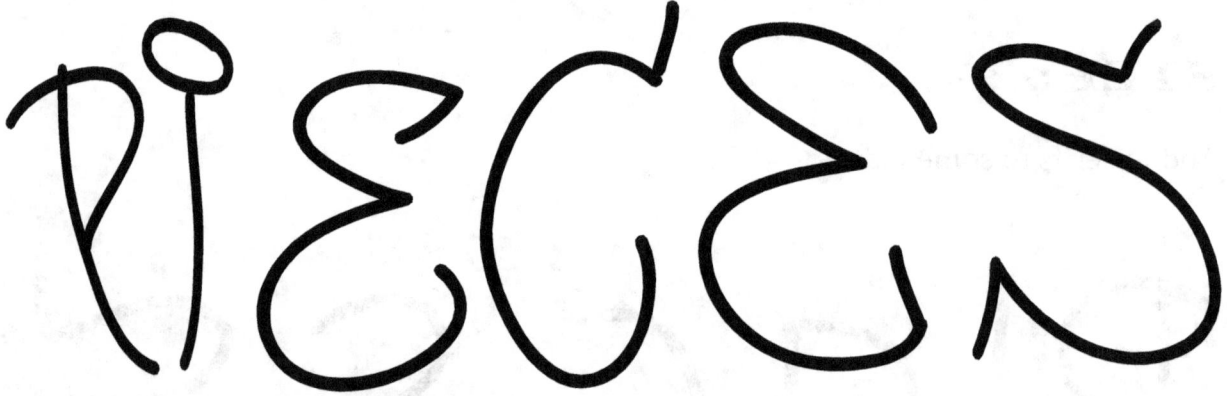

STEP 5

Redraw the letters close in distance overlapping the edges

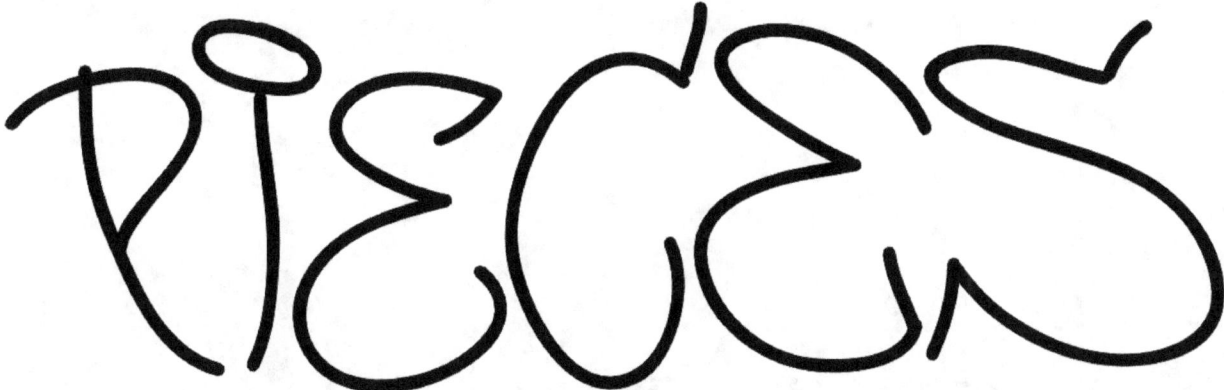

STEP 6

Redraw the letters making the strokes more fluid and add in minor details

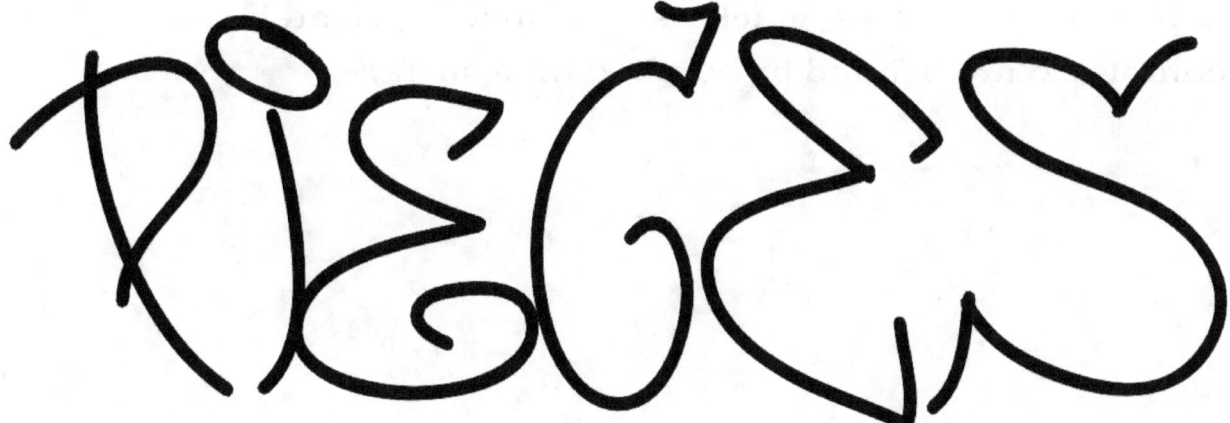

Stickers:

Different from tags, stickers are made privately and when completed are printed or bombed on a surface

how to DRAW a LOS ANGELES TAG

STEP 1

Draw the word STICKERS with straight letters

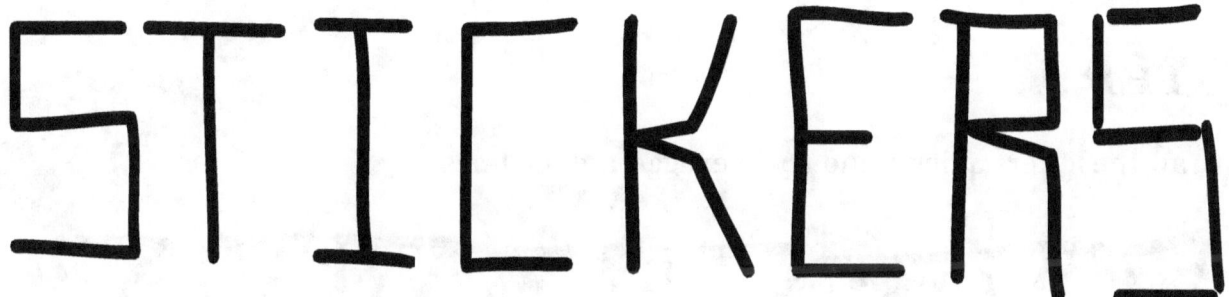

STEP 2

Add in serifs to some letters

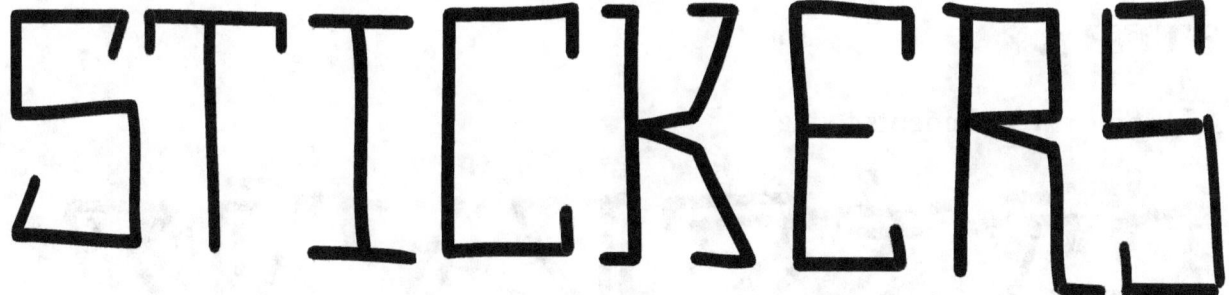

STEP 3

Redraw parts of the tag adding some details to the letters. Blend some lines

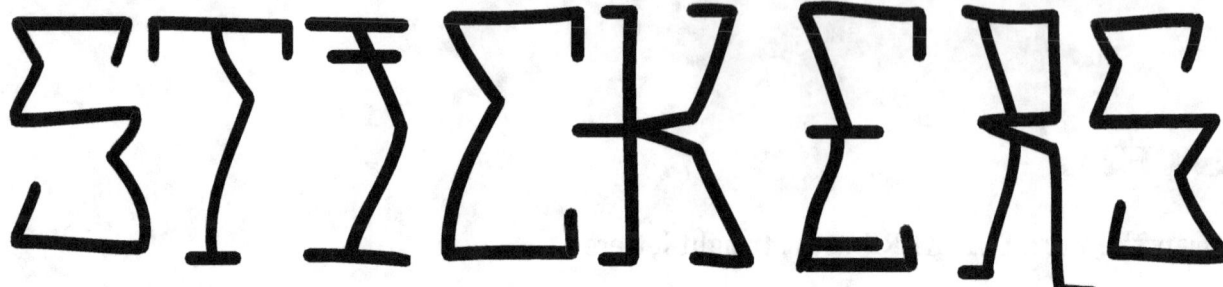

STEP 4

Draw the letters quickly and try to exaggerate the lines

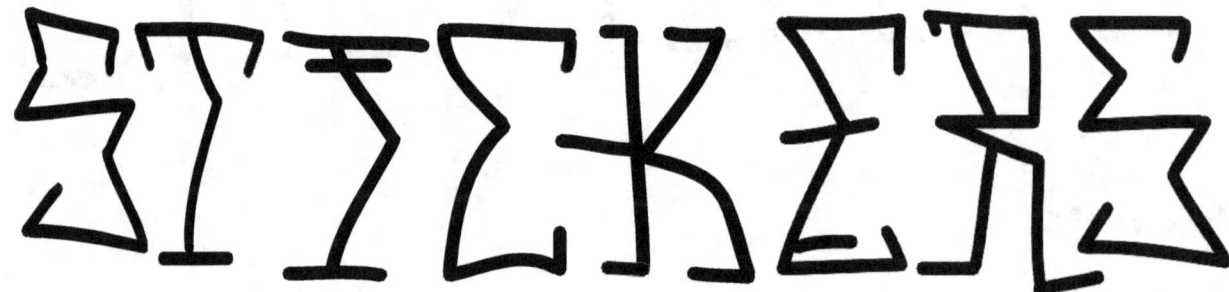

STEP 5

Add some extra elements to tag

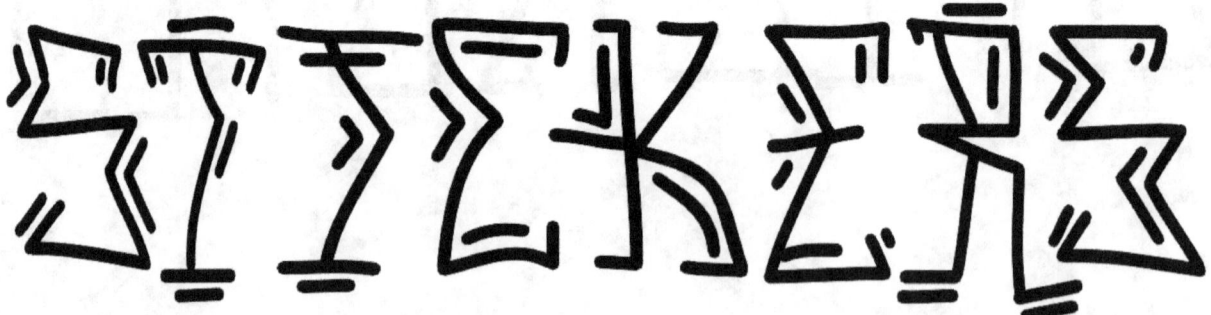

STEP 6

Add an outline with a fine stroke

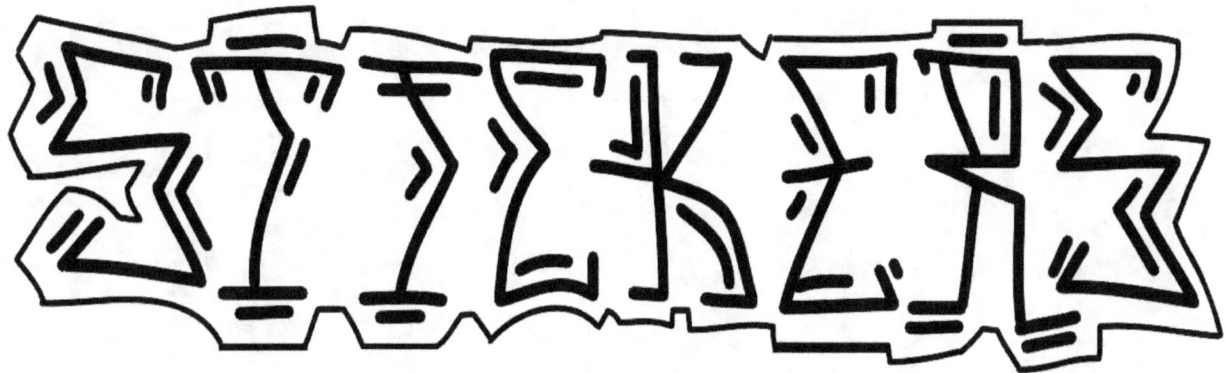

STEP 7

Fill in details to the space between the outline and tag for style

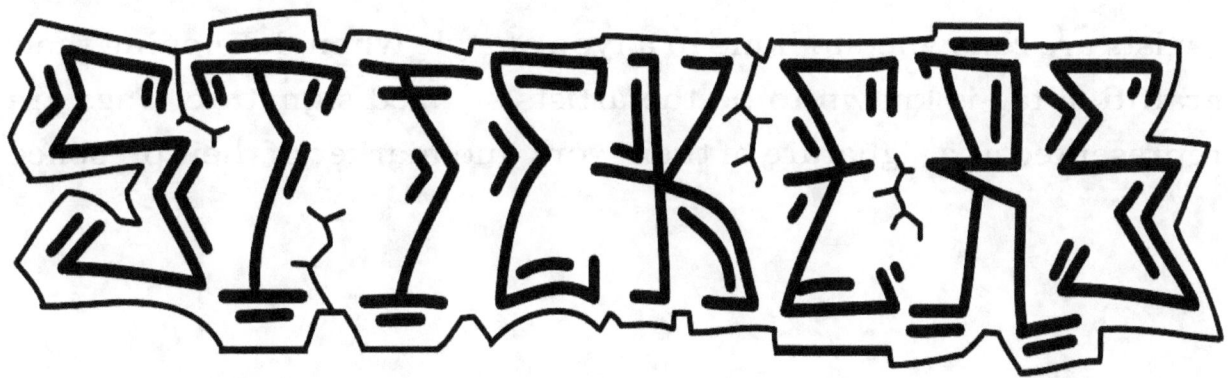

Tags:

Artists are renowned to hone in a type of style when developing their graffiti, a tag is known to be the artists stylized signature. Tags are represented as a signature of their work and marker of their presence

how to DRAW a FREEHAND TAG

STEP 1

Draw the word TAGS with freehand letters

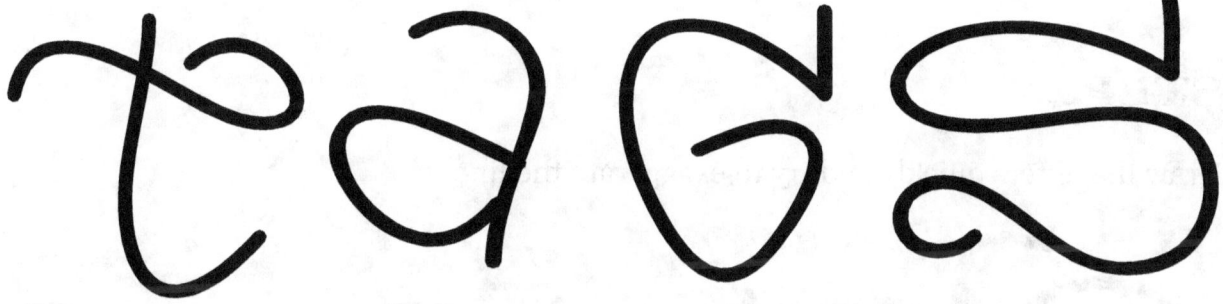

STEP 2

Put the letters together

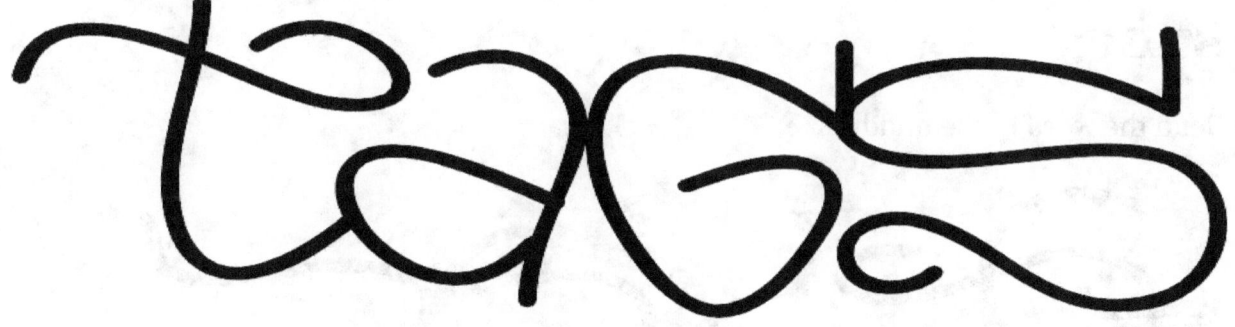

STEP 3

Add in details to the letters like arrows or extensions

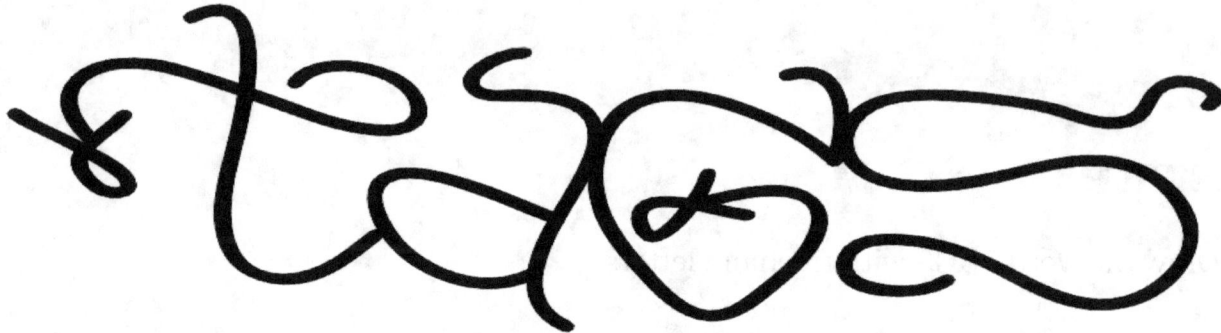

STEP 4

Draw the letters quickly and try to exaggerate the lines

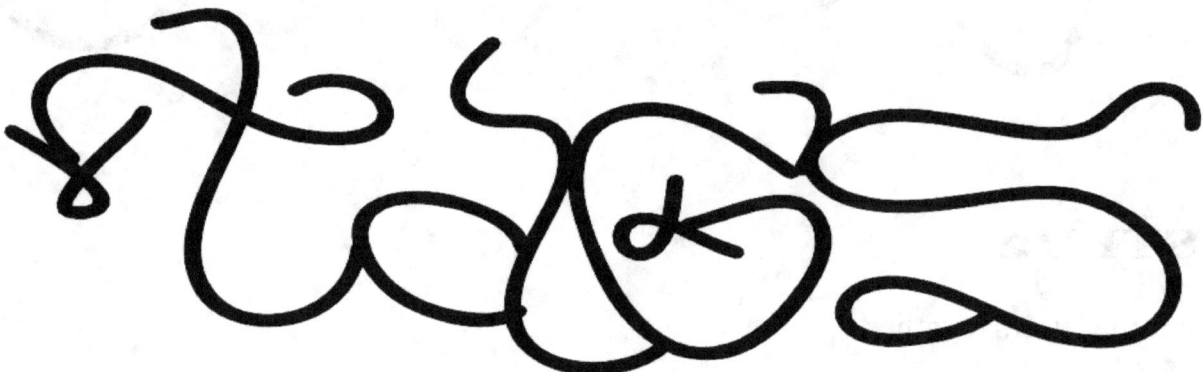

STEP 5

Bend the word in the middle

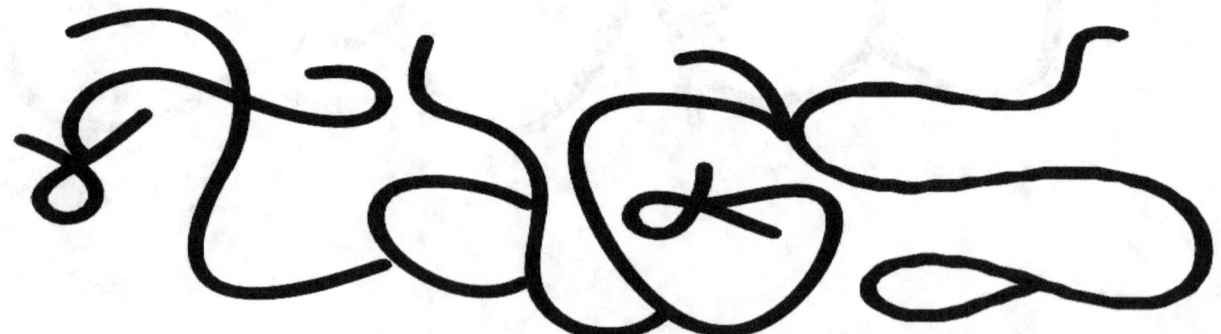

STEP 6

Add extra details like a crown or an asterisk

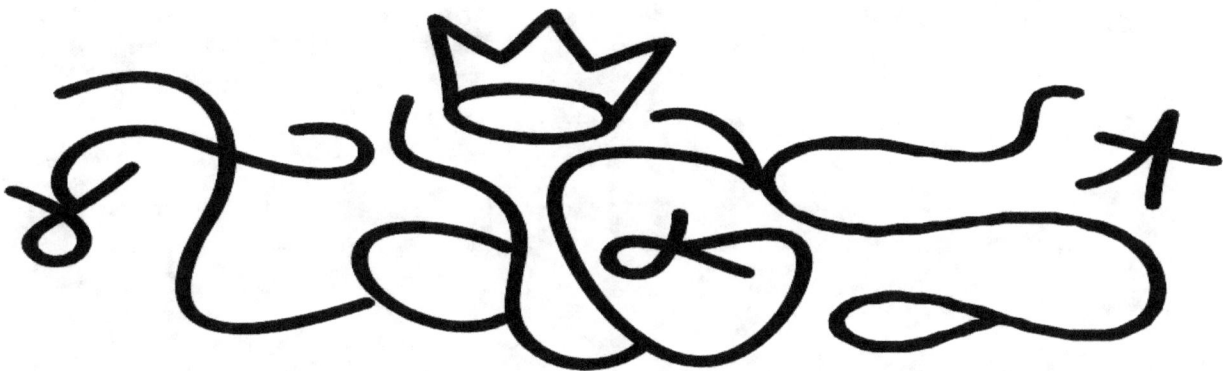

STEP 7

Draw a discontinuous 3D shadow with a fine stroke

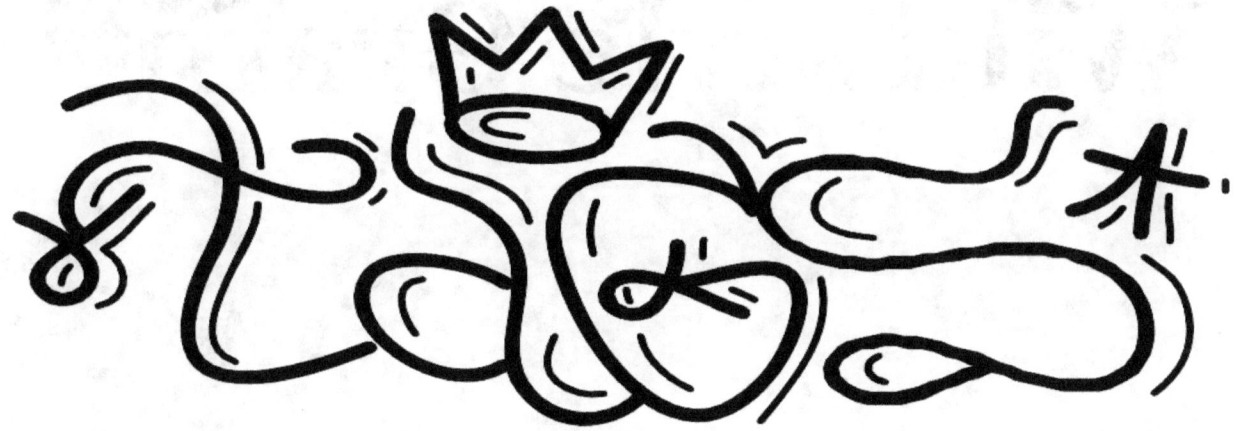

How to Draw a Wild style Graffiti

Background:

Tags aren't set on paper but typically on walls of buildings, trains, non traditional marks. The chosen object to place a piece or tag is known as the background or picture plane.

How to DRAW a
WILDSTYLE GRAFFITI

STEP 1

Draw the word BACKGROUND

BACKGROUND

STEP 2

Draw bars around the lines

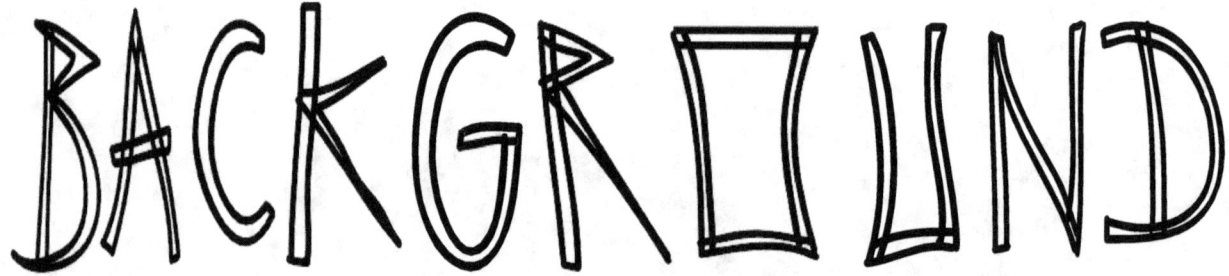

STEP 3

Put the letters together

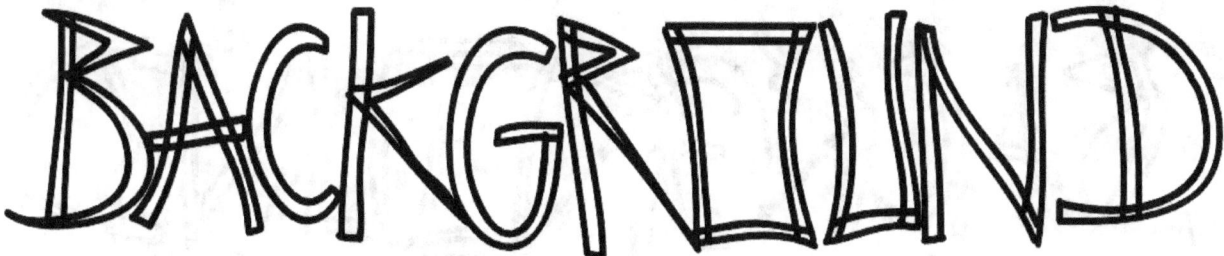

STEP 4

Blend the letters in the same direction

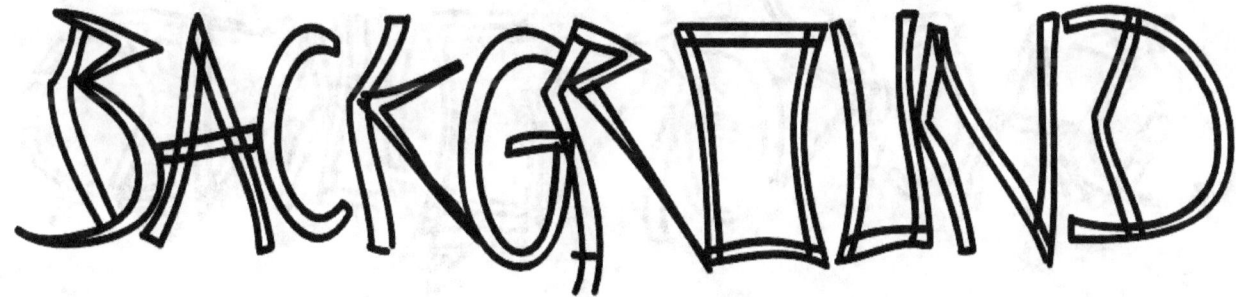

STEP 5

Add serifs to some letters at the top and bottom

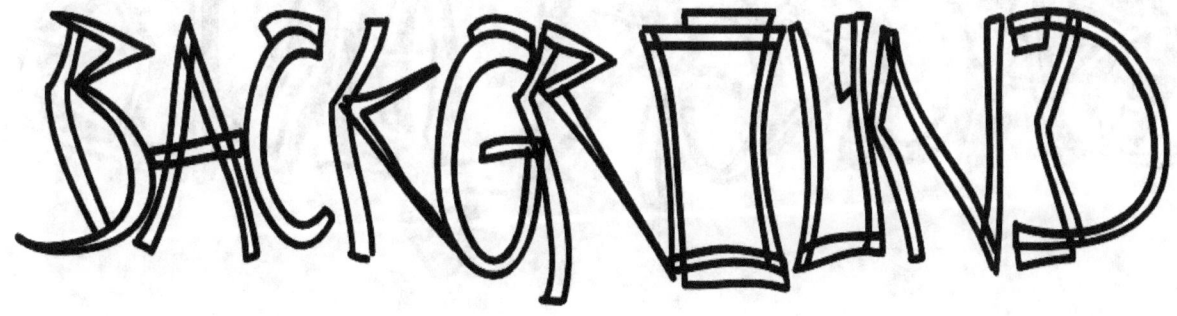

STEP 6

Add arrows to some letters

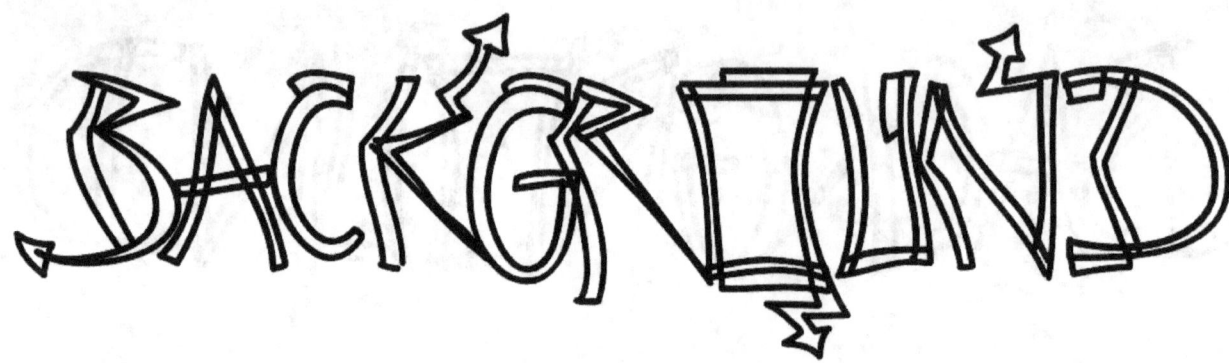

STEP 7

Cut part of some letters in bits

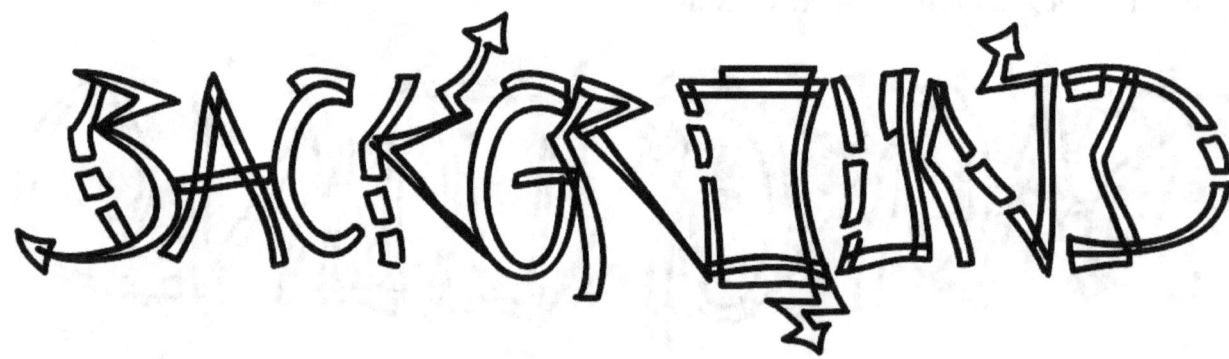

STEP 8

Delete the leftover lines and shade the right-side edges of the letters giving a 3D effect

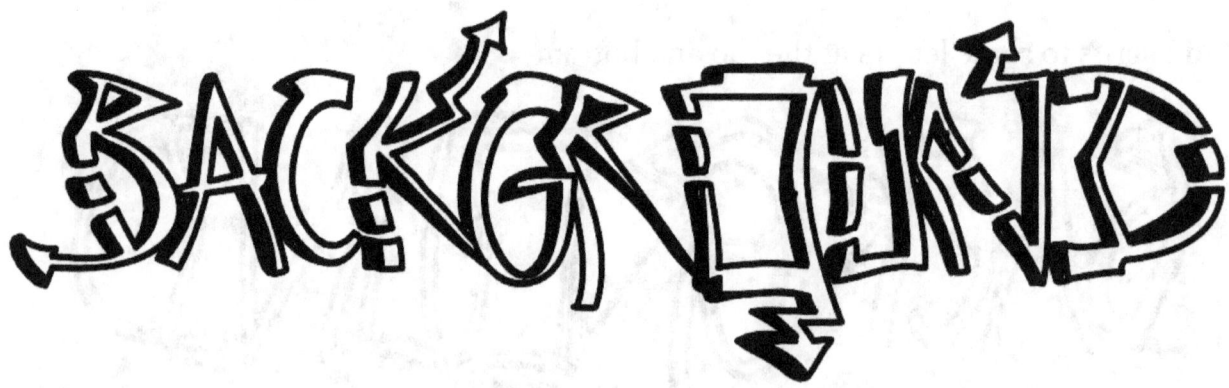

Chromies:

Artists that enjoy developing throwups, multiple tags in links in heloc shape

how to DRAW a WILDSTYLE GRAFFITI

STEP 1

Draw the word CHROMIES in tag style

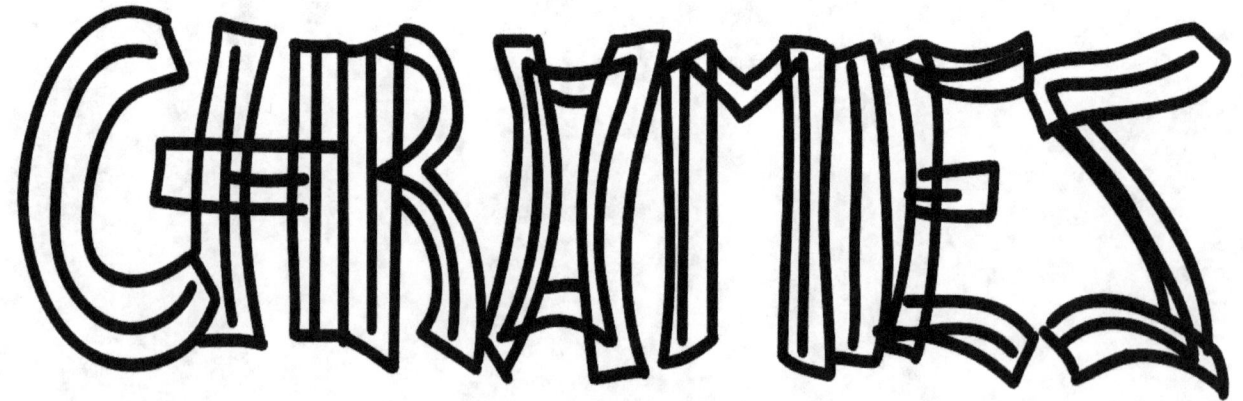

STEP 2

Draw bars around the lines

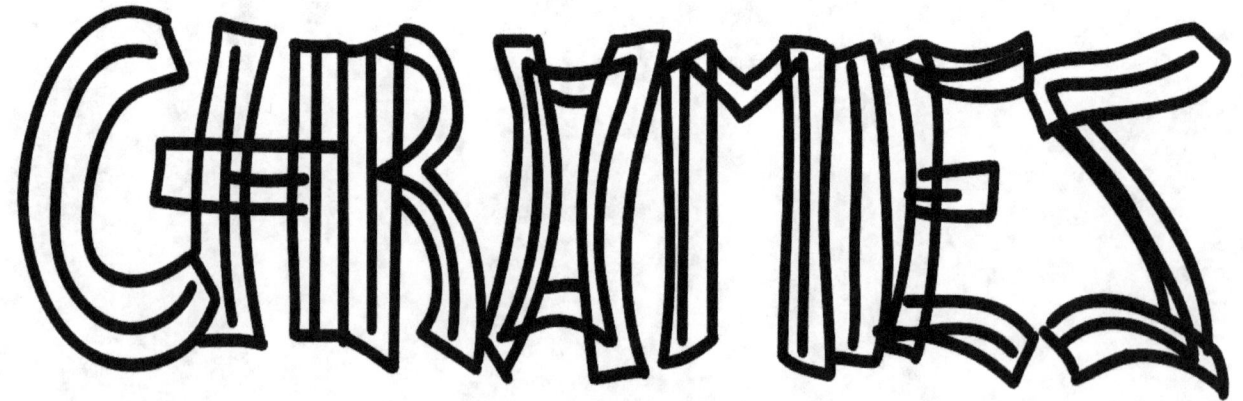

STEP 3

Blend the letters in alternate directions and erase the inside lines

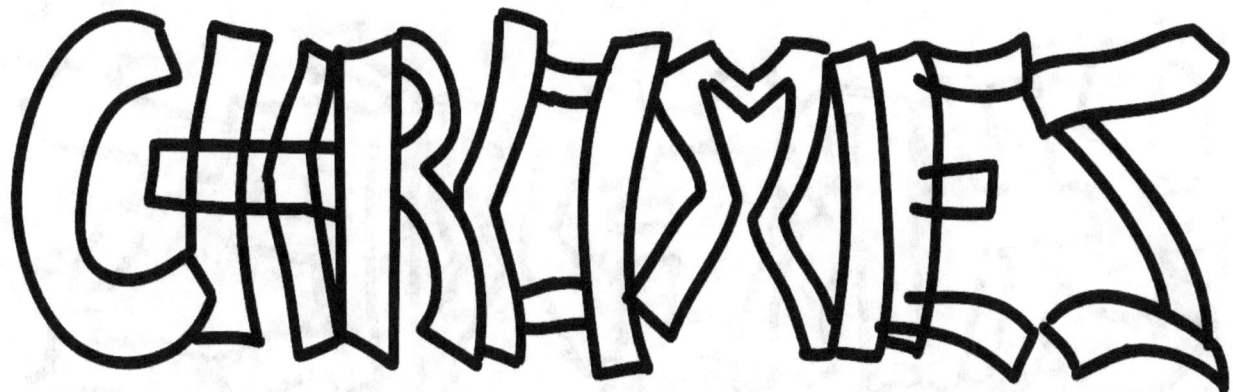

STEP 4

Draw in serifs and arrows to some letters

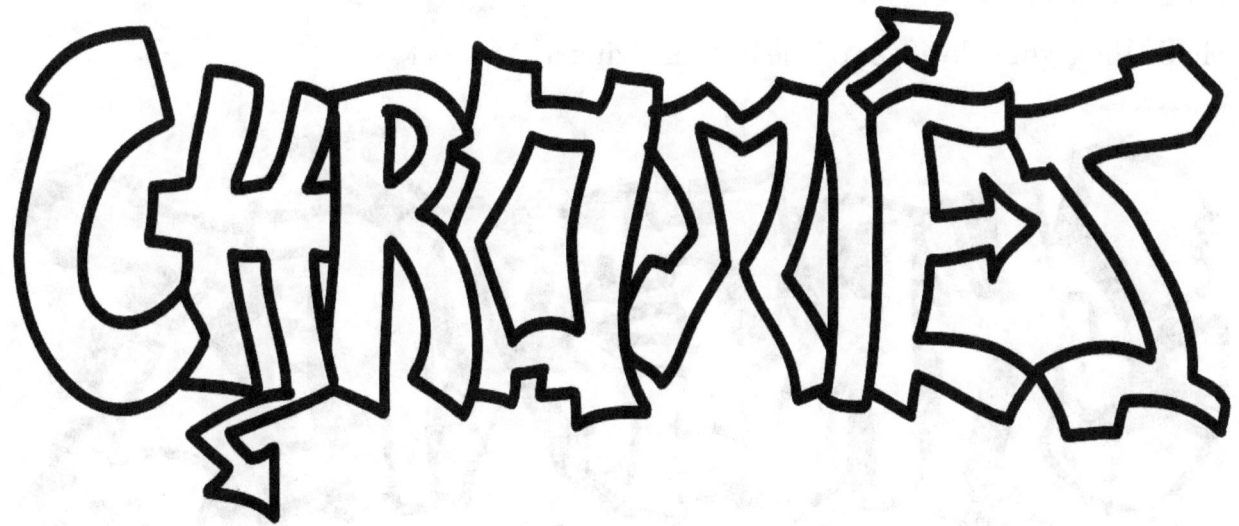

STEP 5

Cut part of some letters in bits

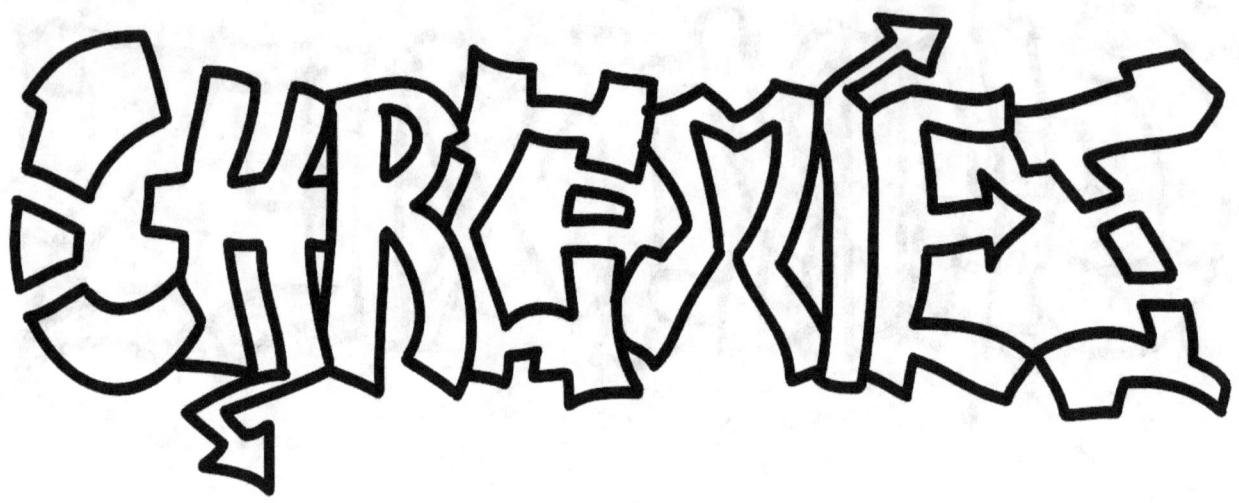

STEP 6

Shade the right side edges of the letters giving a 3D effect

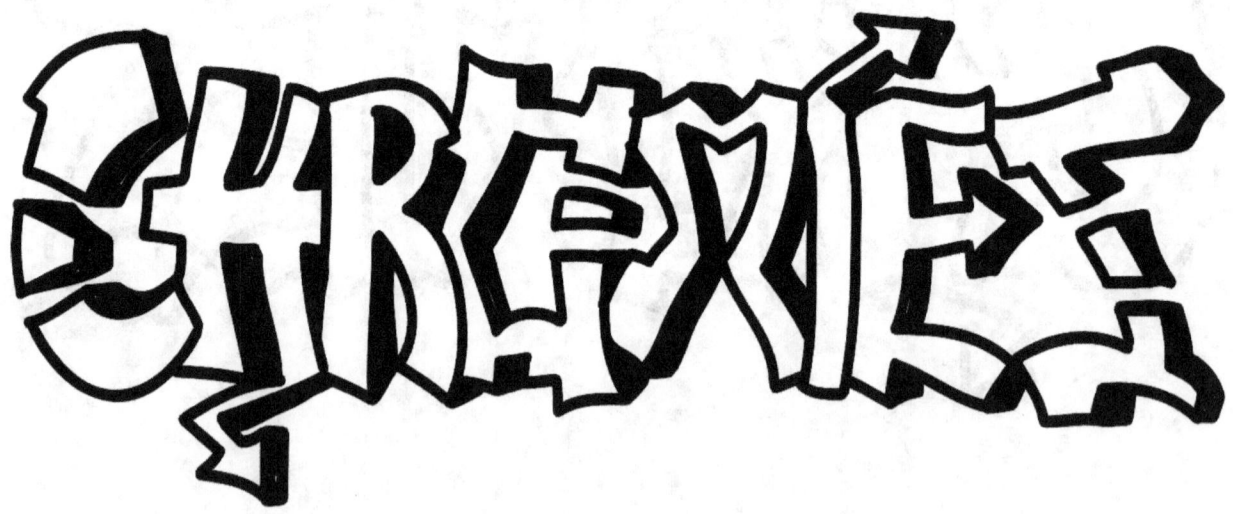

Hollows:

A graffiti piece that contains no fill but consists of only an outline. Aesthetically different piece

how to DRAW a WILDSTYLE GRAFFITI

STEP 1

Draw the word Hollows with swirling strokes to add tag style

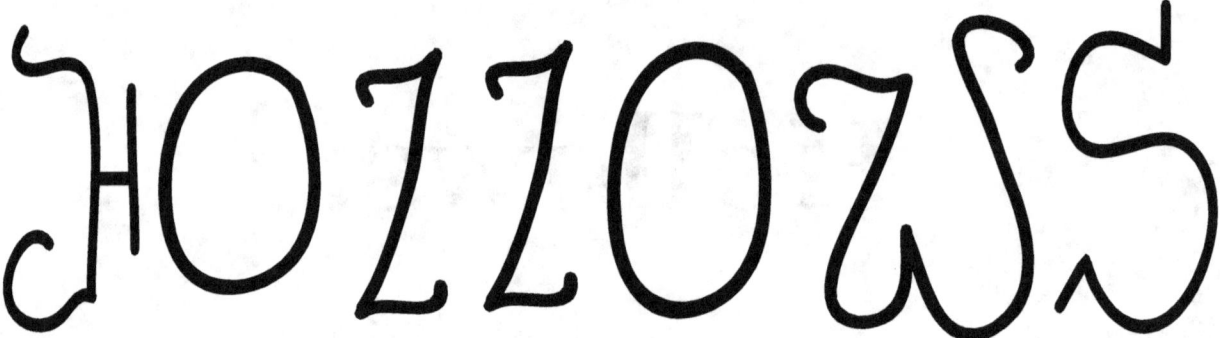

STEP 2

Draw bars around the lines

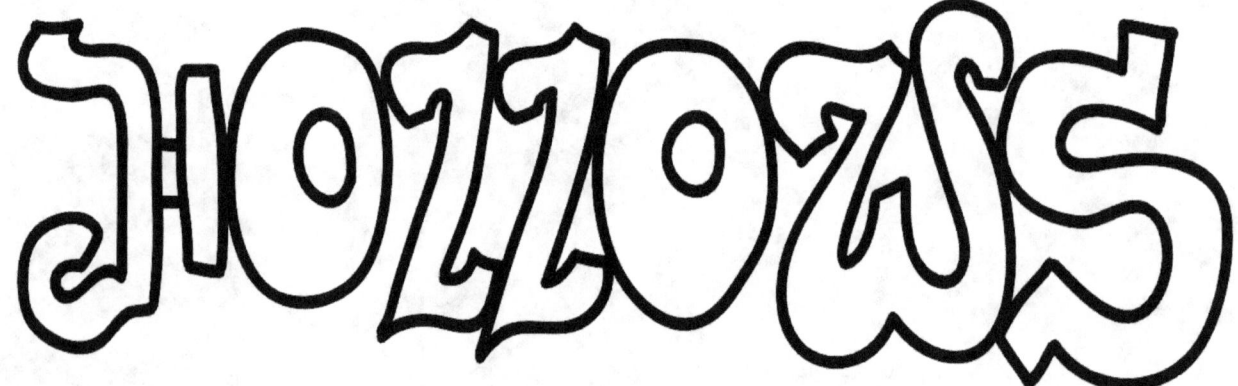

STEP 3

Now blend each bar in one or more places

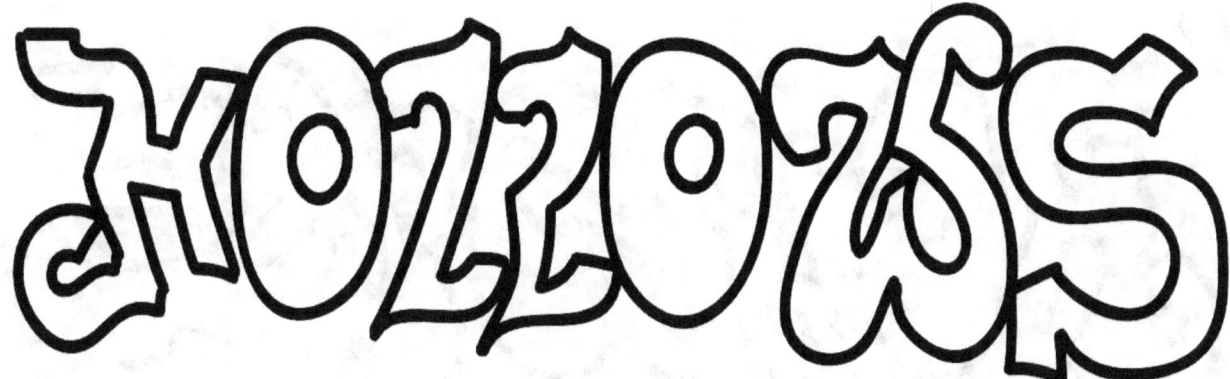

STEP 4

Draw in extensions and arrows to the letters

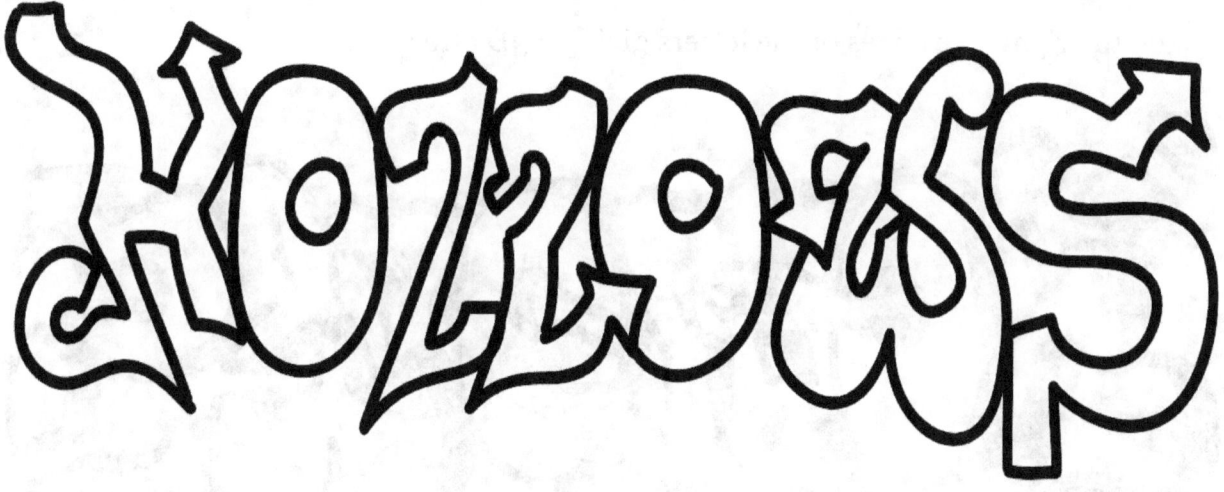

STEP 5

Cut part of some letters in bits

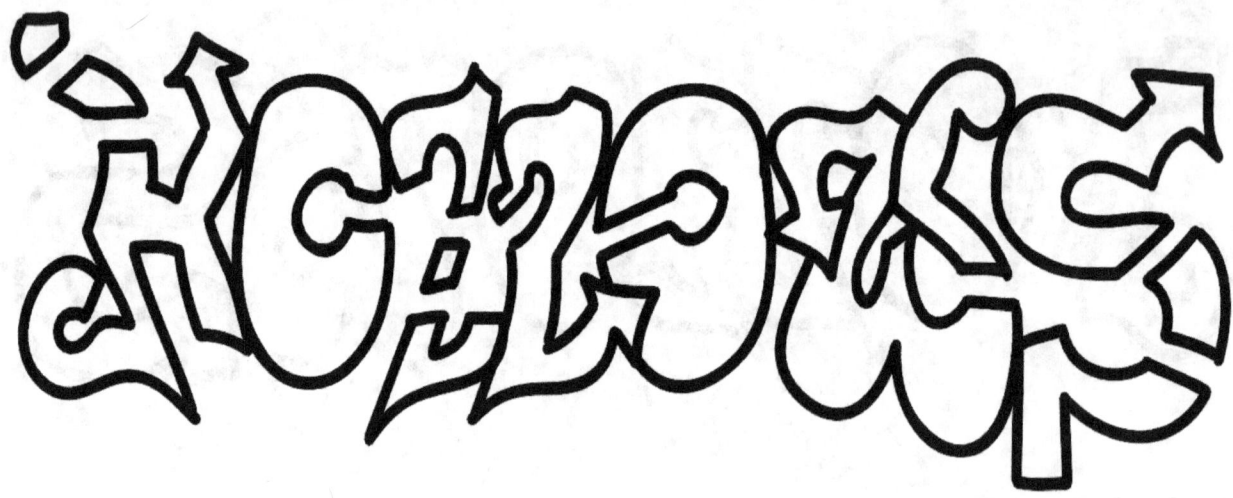

STEP 6

Shade the right side edges of the letters giving a 3D effect

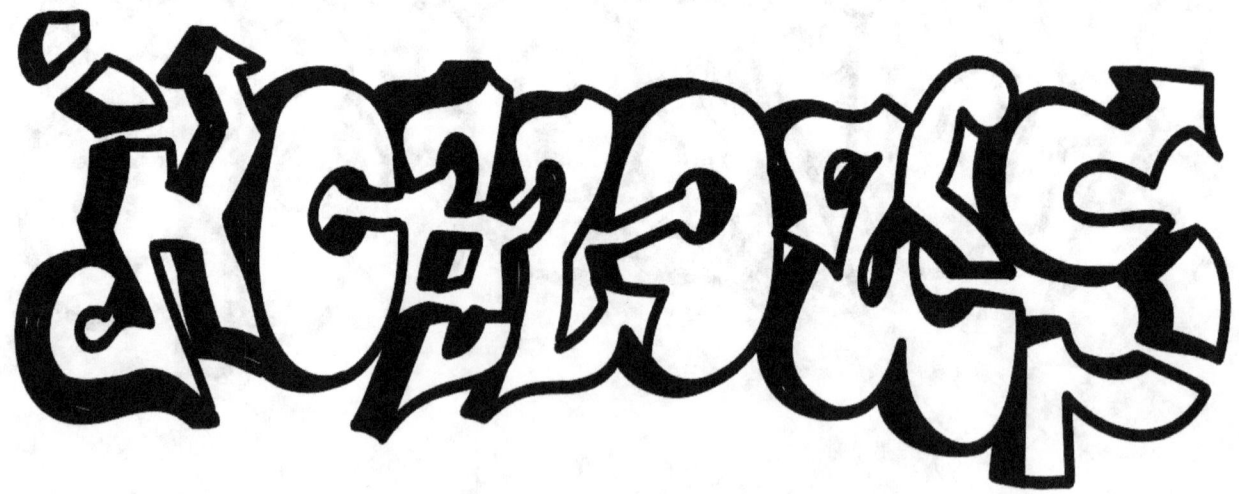

Keyline:

On the outside of a piece there is a line that runs through through the piece known as a keyline

how to DRAW a WILDSTYLE GRAFFITI

STEP 1

Draw the word KEYLINE in tagstyle

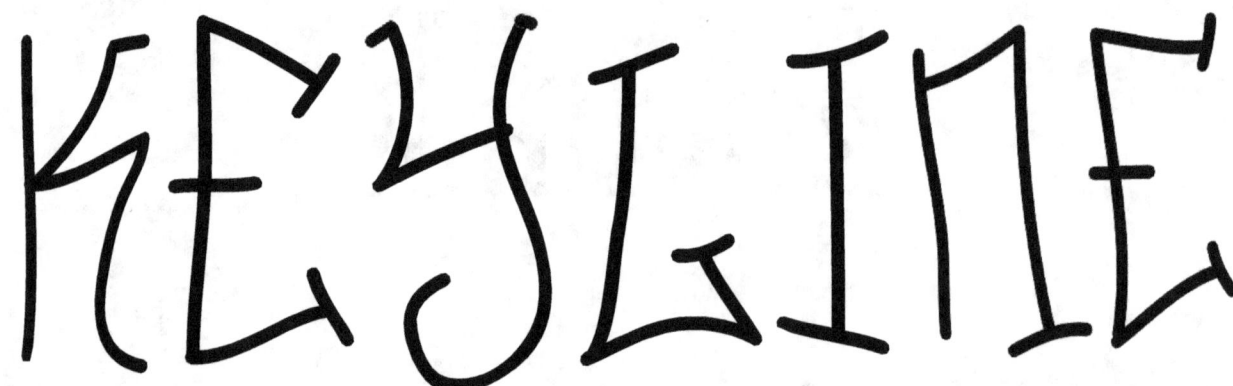

STEP 2

Draw bars around the lines

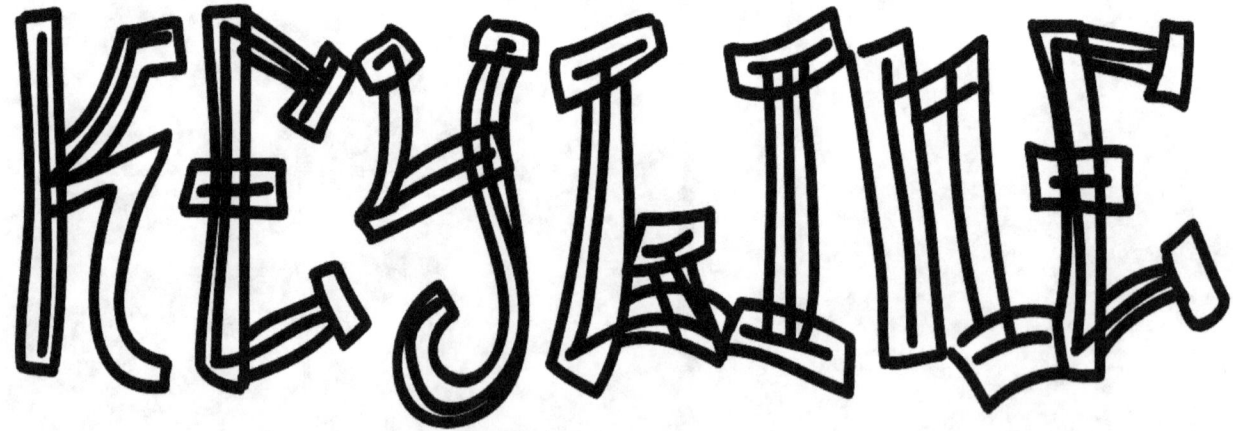

STEP 3

Delete the inside lines and blend some bars

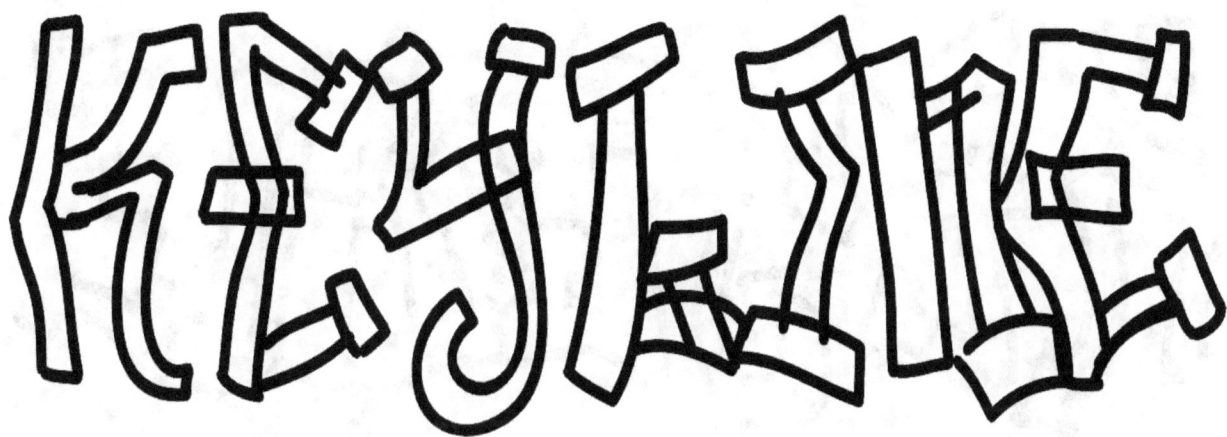

STEP 4

Draw in serifs and arrows to some letters

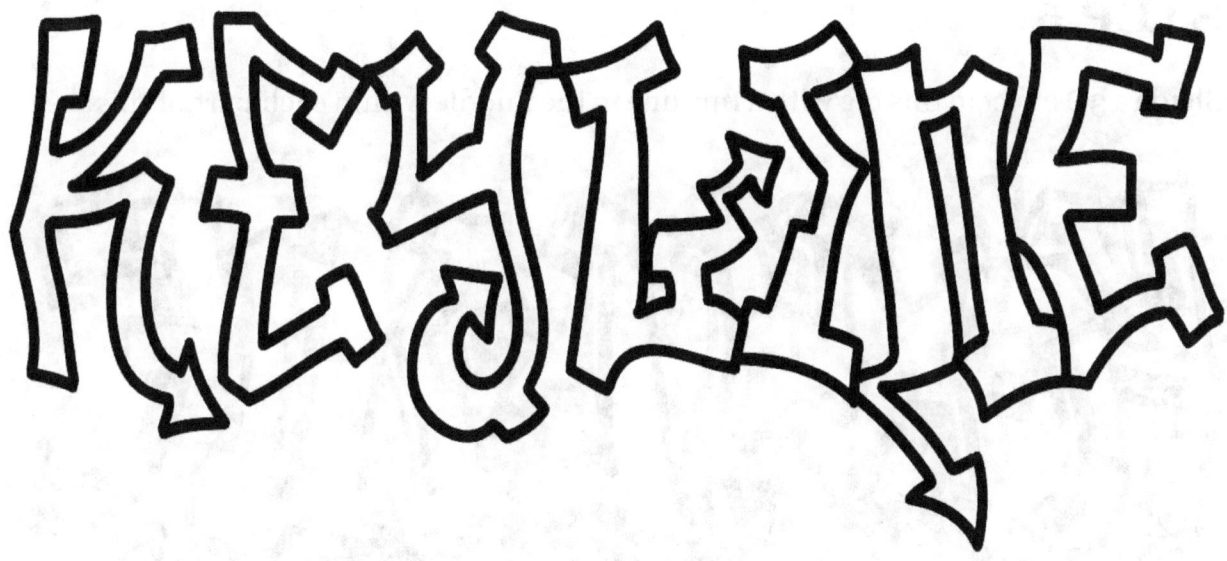

STEP 5

Make some lines crossing the letters

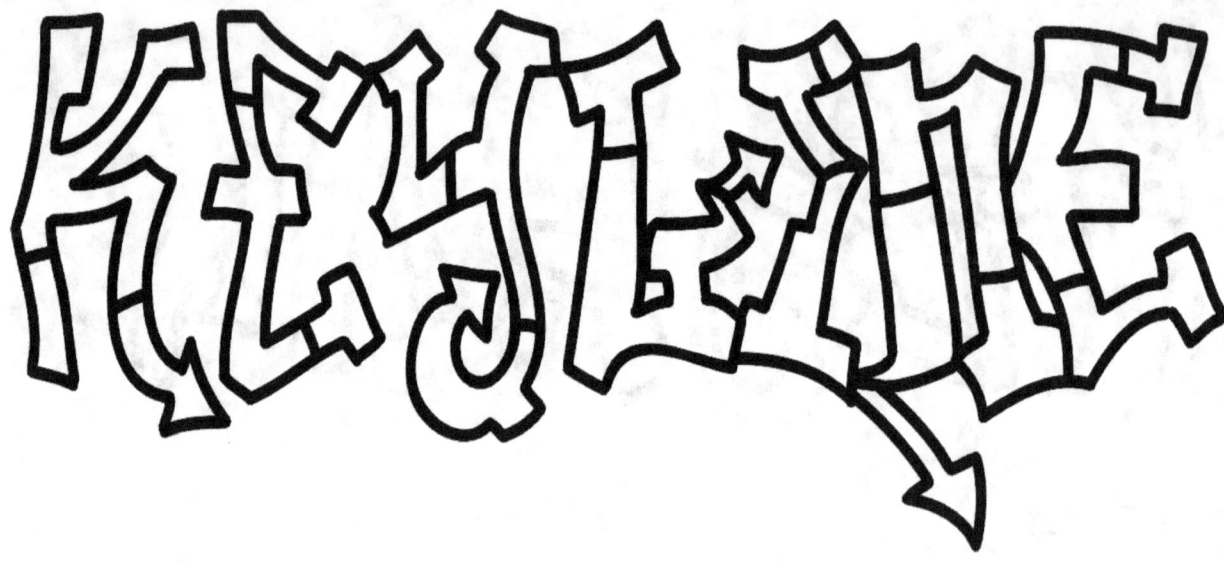

STEP 6

Shade a 3D effect in this tag with a fine line in the middle within each part of this area

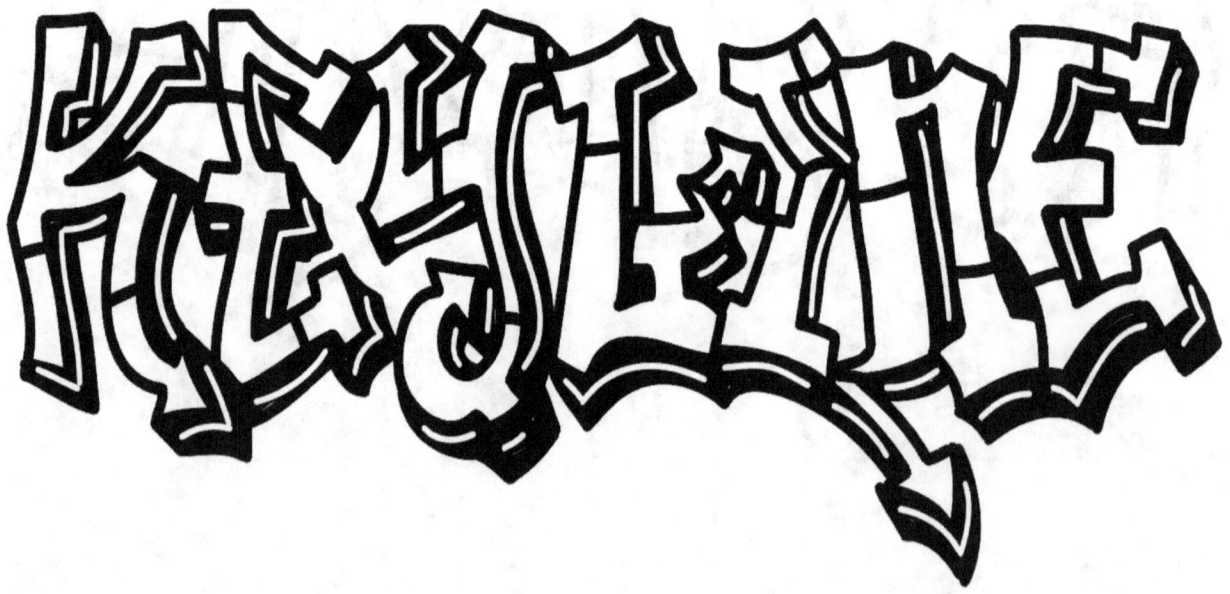

Scribe:

To scribe is referred to as scratching a surface typically a window to create a tag using objects such as a knife, stone, key etc. A scribe is hard to remove

how to DRAW a WILDSTYLE GRAFFITI

STEP 1

Draw the word SCRIBE in tagstyle

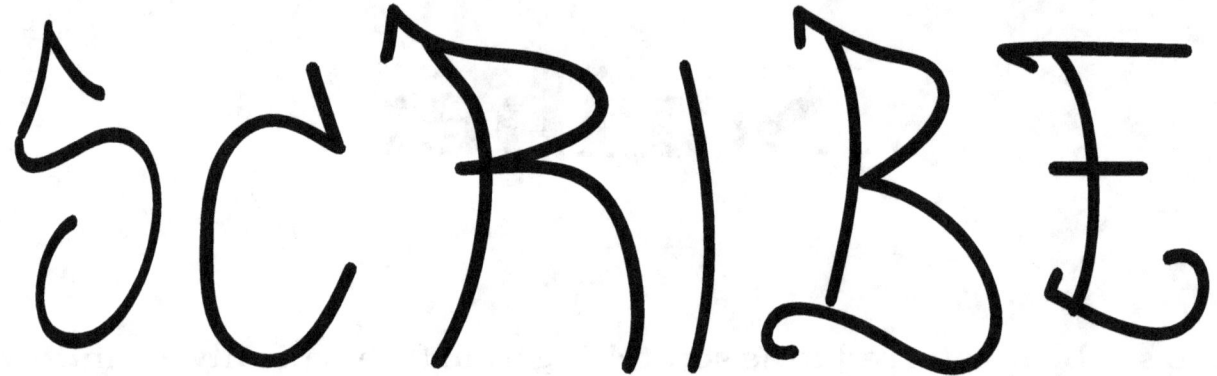

STEP 2

Move the letters up or down

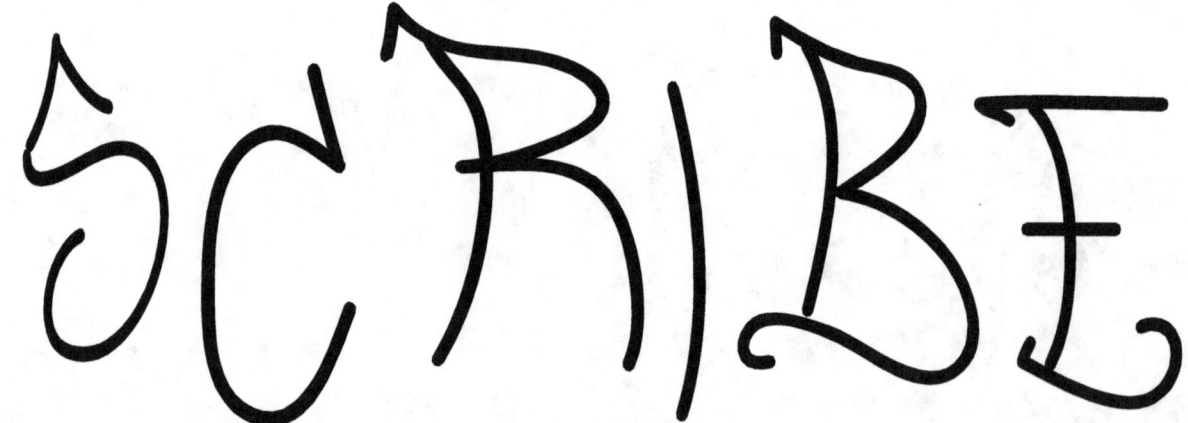

STEP 3

Put the letters together and draw bars around them

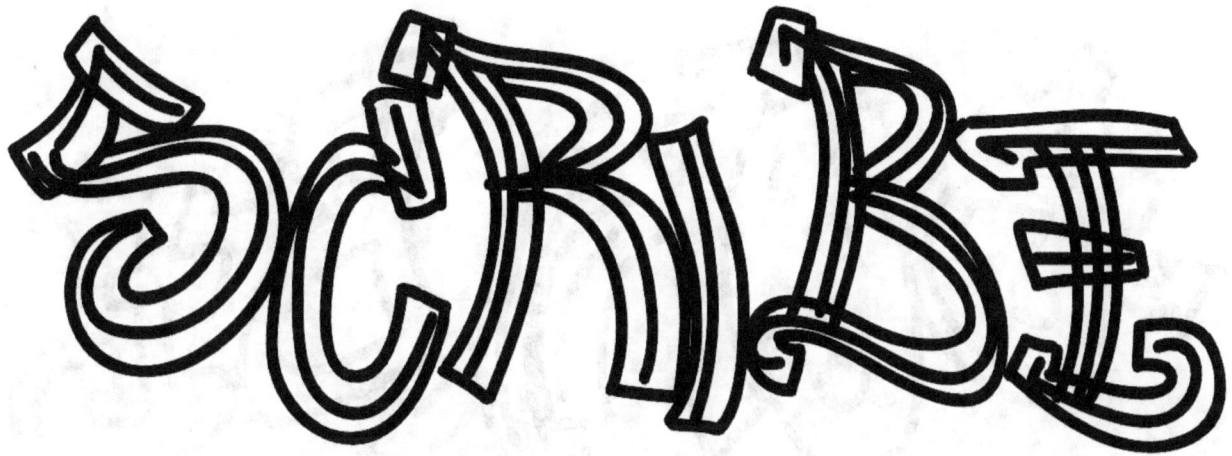

STEP 4

Erase the inside lines and add in serifs and arrows to some letters

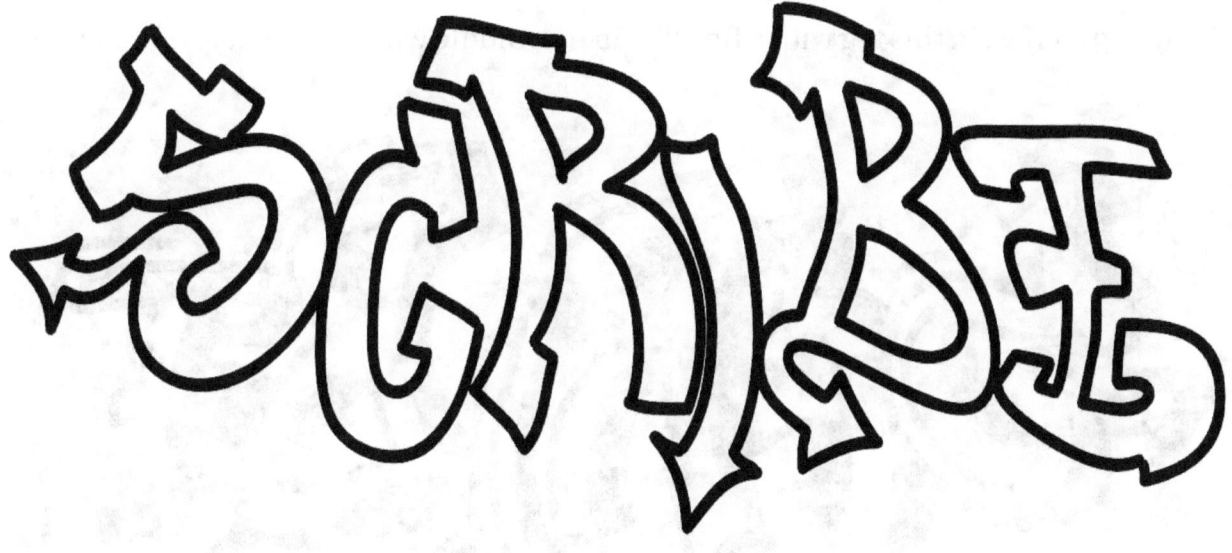

STEP 5

Add in lines with a point inside of the letters near the principal lines

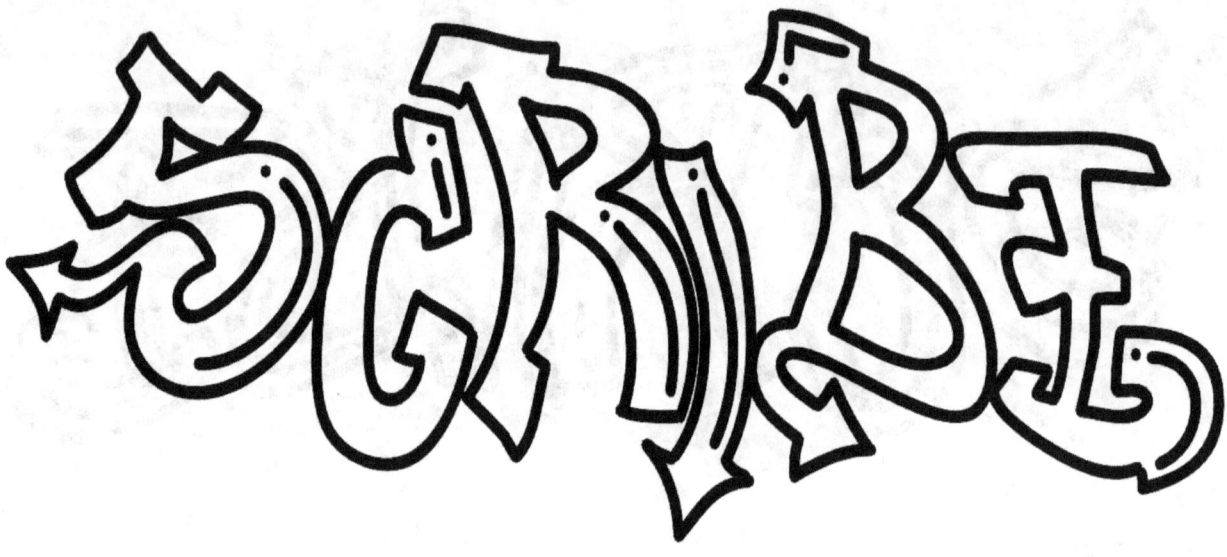

STEP 6

Shade a 3D effect in this tag with a fine line in the middle within each part of this area

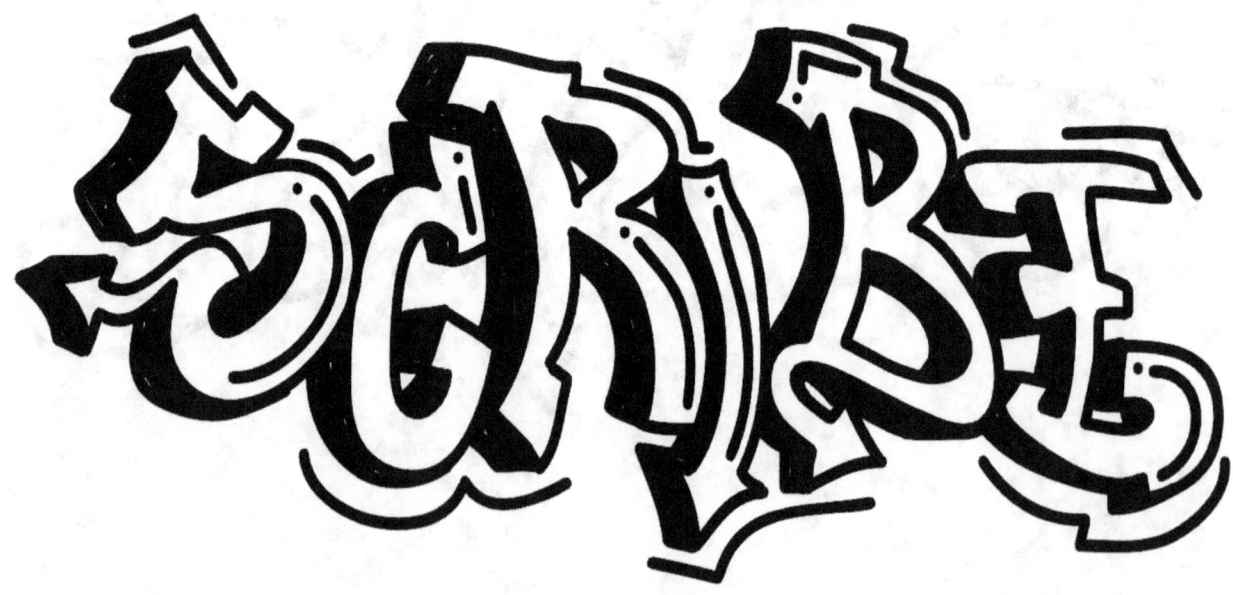

Vandalism:

Graffiti on a property without the owners consent is referred to as vandalism. Many run the risk of police arrest for this so be careful where you exhibit your art

how to DRAW a WILDSTYLE GRAFFITI

STEP 1

Draw the word VANDALISM

VANDALISM

STEP 2

Draw bars around the lines

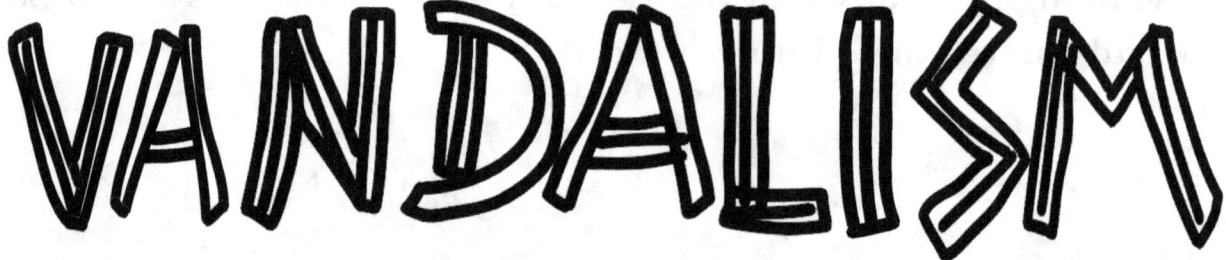

STEP 3

Put the letters together

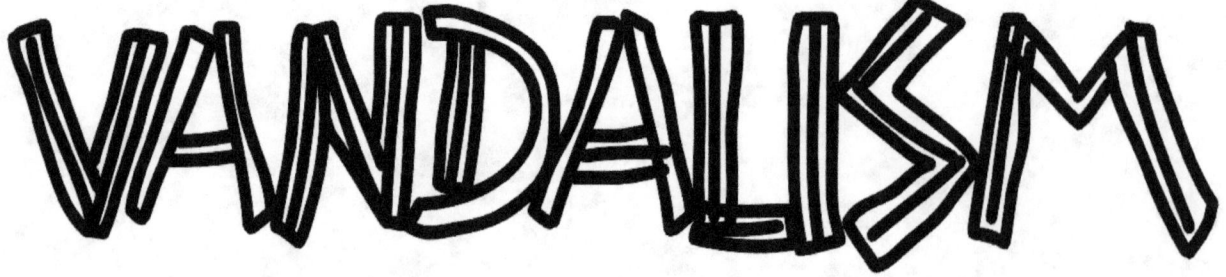

STEP 4

Blend the letters in the same direction and erase the inside lines

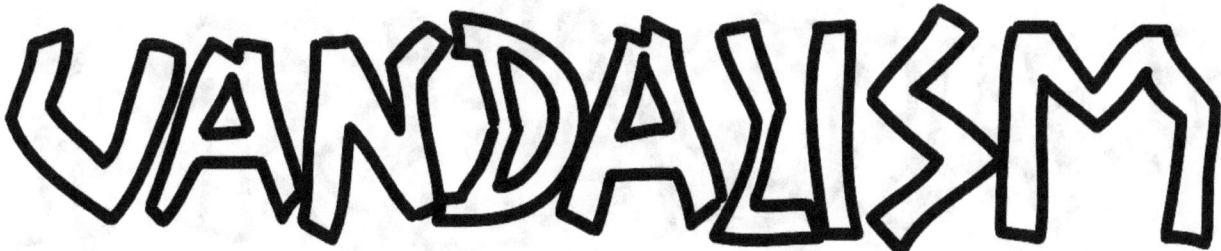

STEP 5

Draw in serifs and arrows to some letters

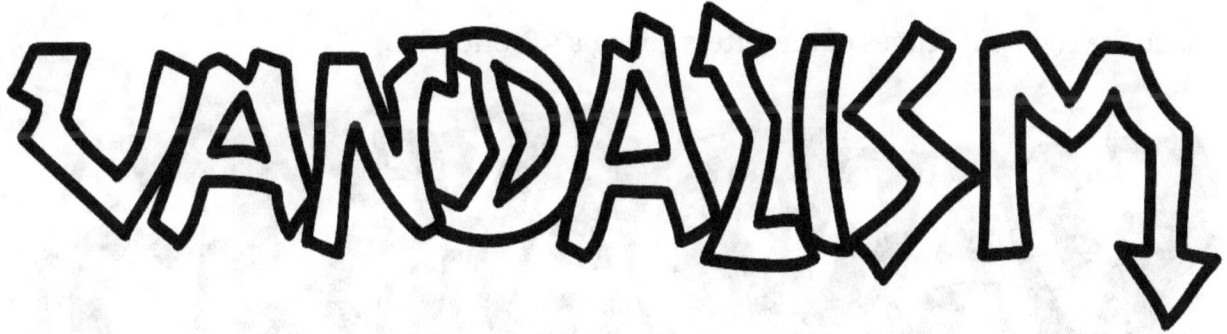

STEP 6

Cut part of some letters in bits

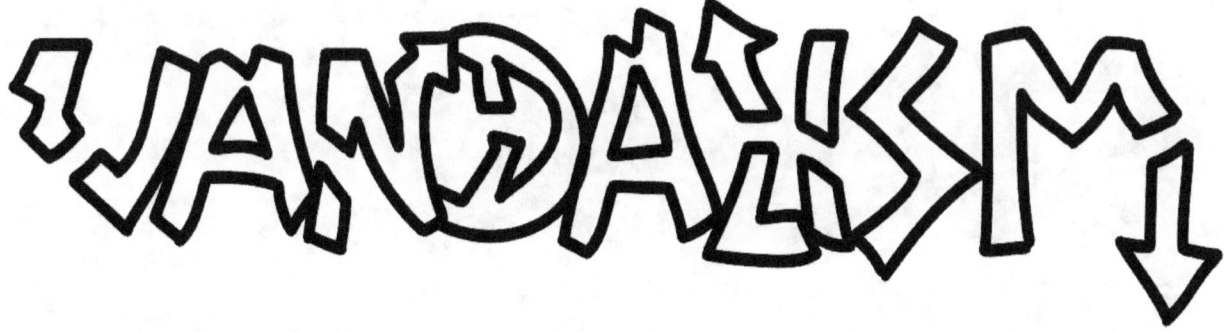

STEP 7

Make some line crossing the letters

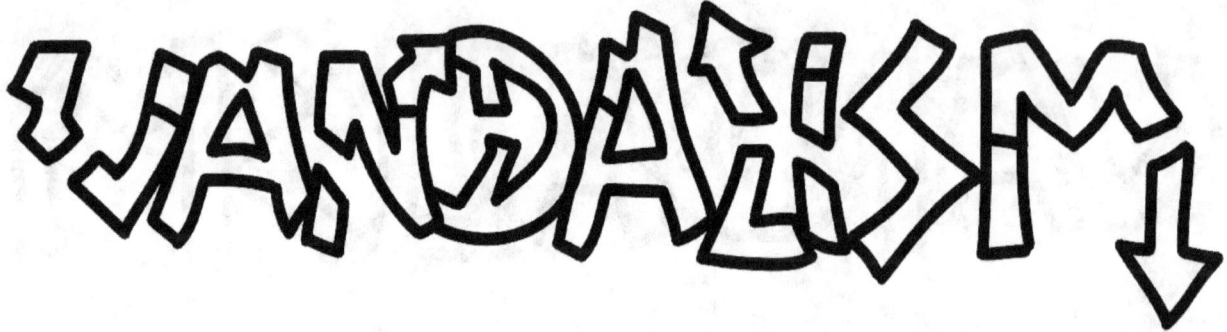

STEP 8

Shade the right-side edges of the letters giving a 3D effect

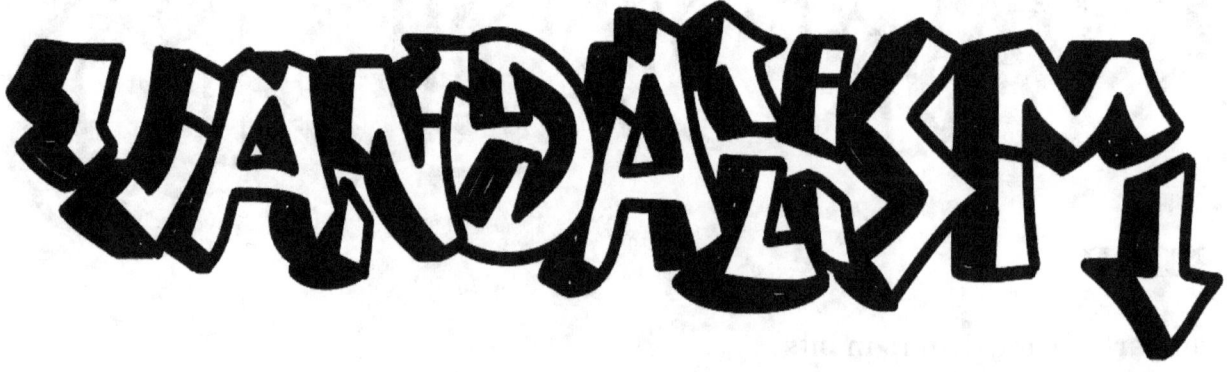

Wildstyle:

A style of graffiti that is described as an interlocking type of calligraphy

how to DRAW a WILDSTYLE GRAFFITI

STEP 1

Draw the word WILDSTYLE in lower case letters

wildstyle

STEP 2

Draw bars around the lines

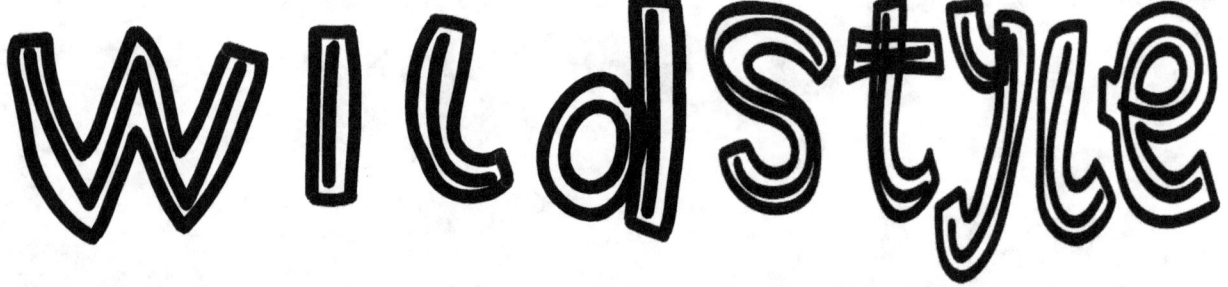

STEP 3

Put the letters together and draw bars around them

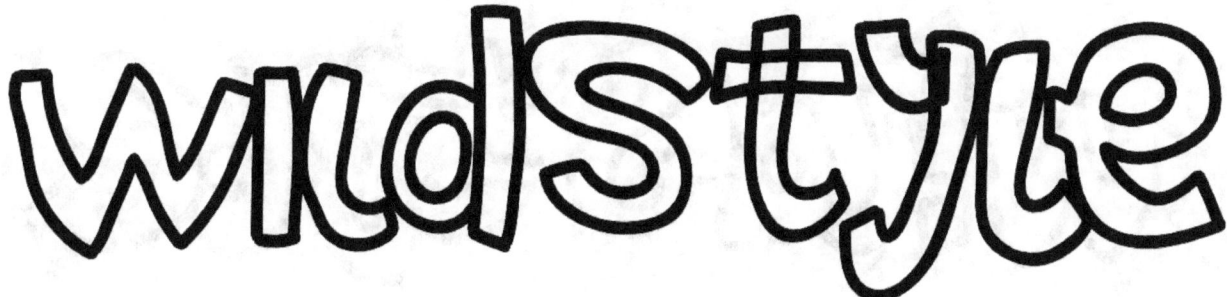

STEP 4

Blend some bars in the same direction

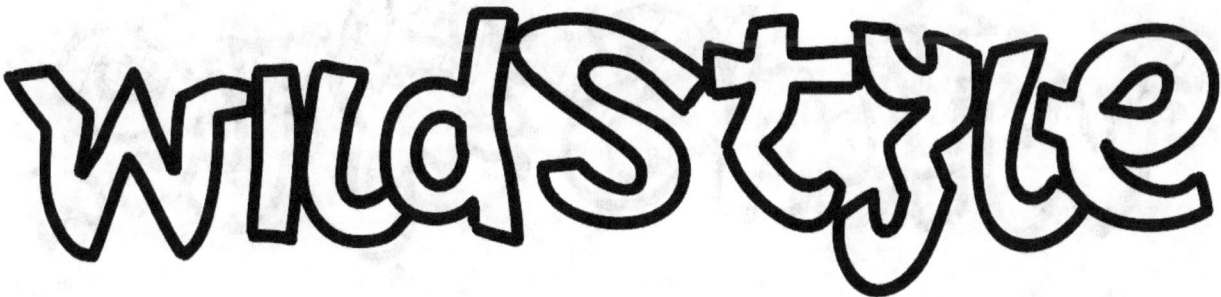

STEP 5

Redraw by flattening or reducing some bars and adding arrows

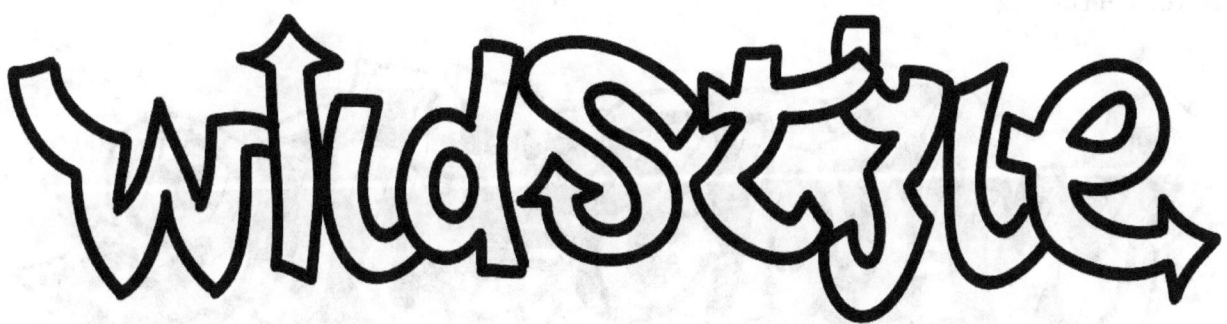

STEP 6

Cut part of some letters in bits

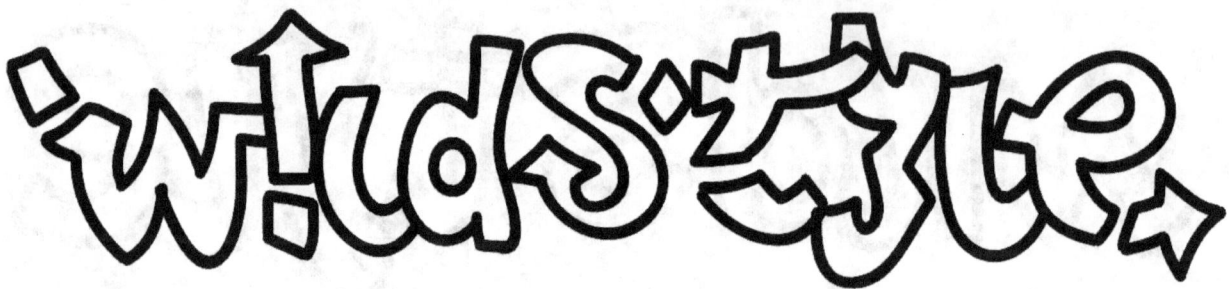

STEP 7

Add diagonal lines from middle to top of letters with a fine stroke

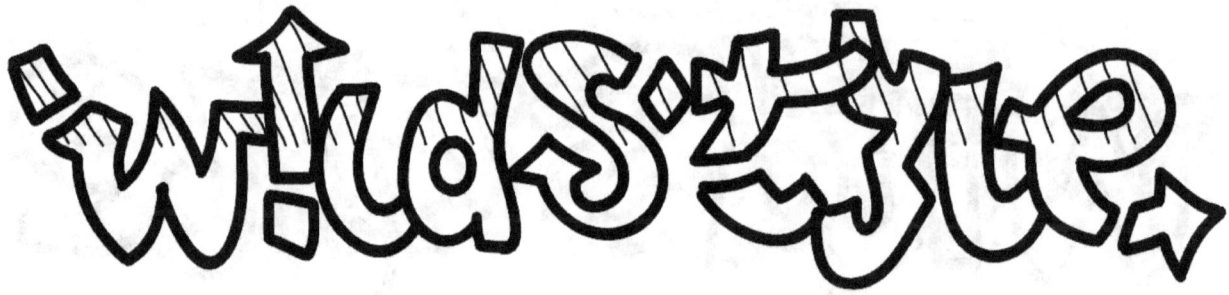

STEP 8

Shade the right side edges of the letters giving a 3D effect along with drawing a continuous line around the letters of the tag with drawing a continuous line around the letters of the tag

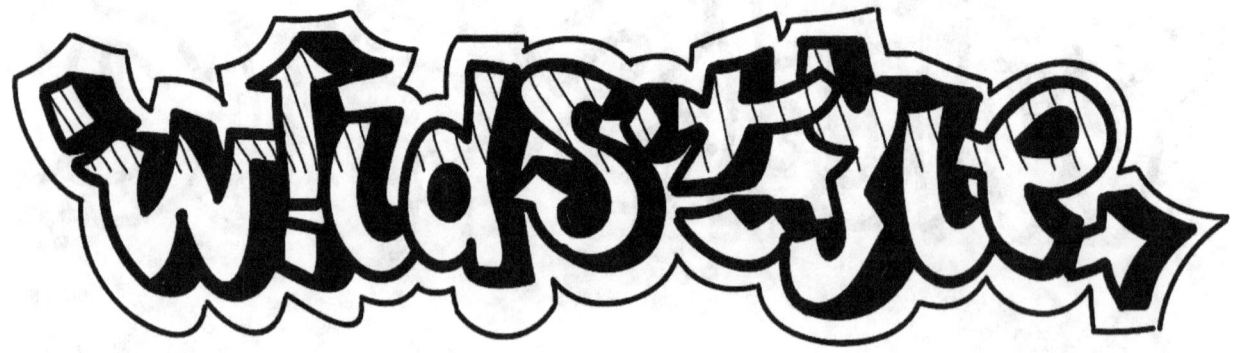

How To Draw a Bubble Graffiti/ Urban Lettering

Aerosol:

Imagery type of art such as cartoons or comic book character designs that are incorporated into the design

how to DRAW a BUBBLE GRAFFITI

STEP 1

Draw the word AEROSOL with lower case letters

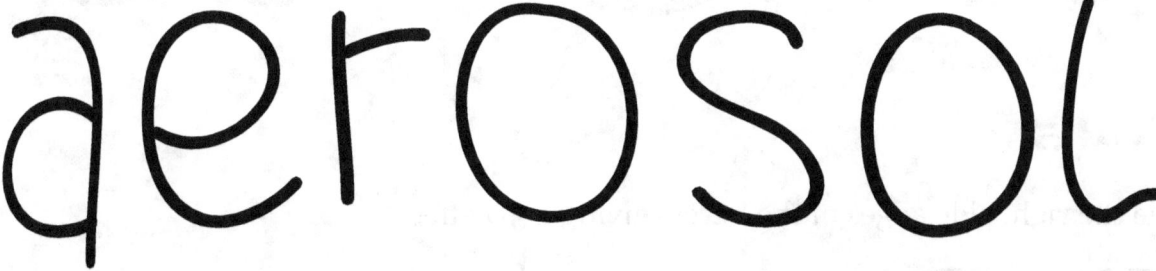

STEP 2

Now draw an outline around the letters with the size you want

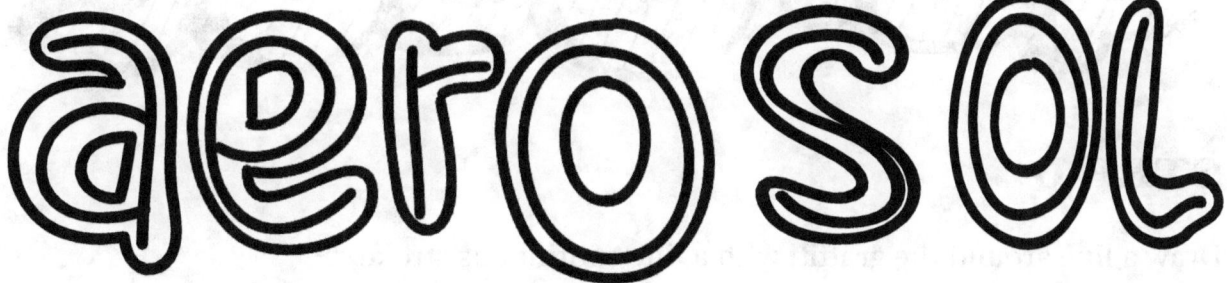

STEP 3

Put the letters together and erase the inside lines

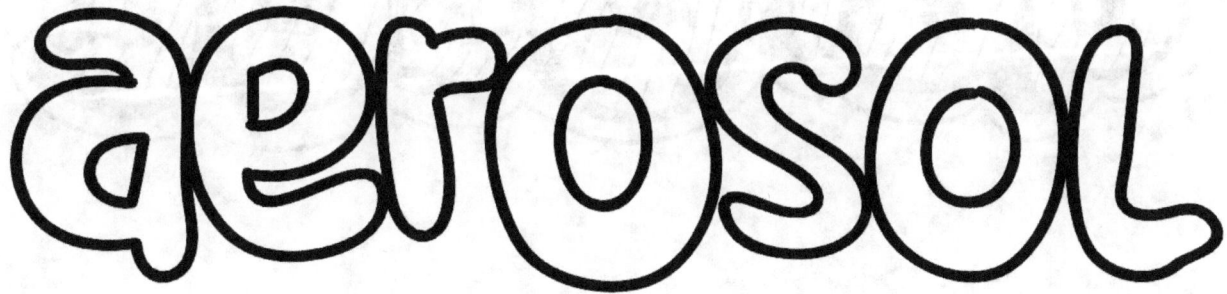

STEP 4

Add nearby diagonal lines half down within the letters with very fine strokes

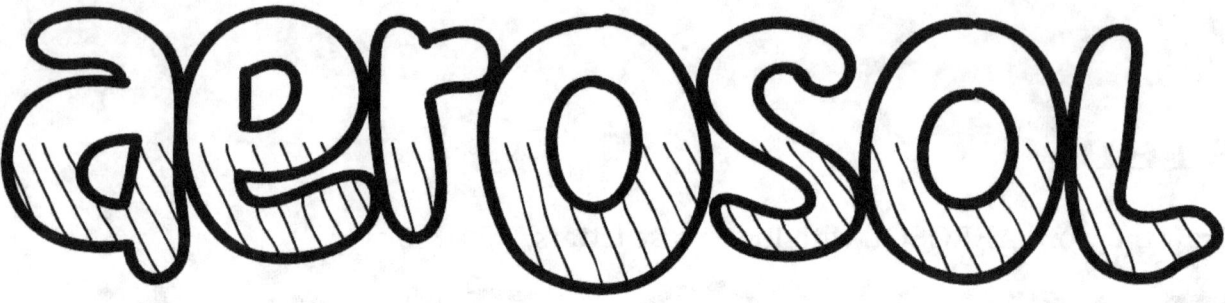

STEP 5

Shade the right side edges of the letters giving a 3D effect

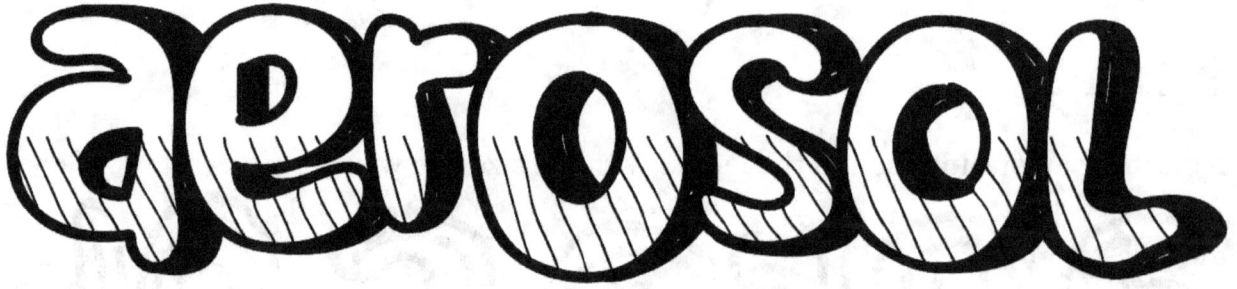

STEP 6

Draw a line around the graffiti with a fine continuous stroke

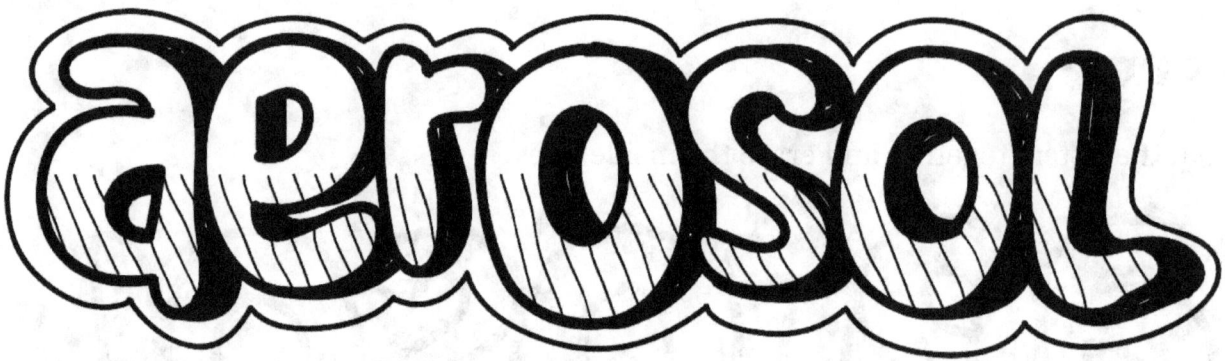

Bombing:

When you are producing mass amount of graffiti in an area you are bombing

how to DRAW a BUBBLE GRAFFITI

STEP 1

Draw the word BOMBING

BOMBING

STEP 2

Simulate a tag, making variations in the letters

BOMBING

STEP 3

Draw around the outside and inside edges around the letters

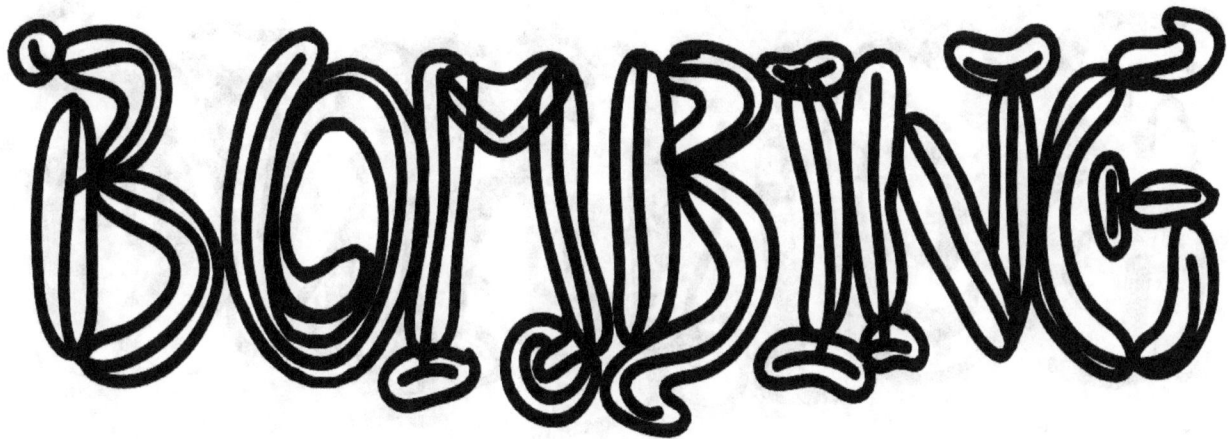

STEP 4

Redraw the letters close in distance overlapping the edges

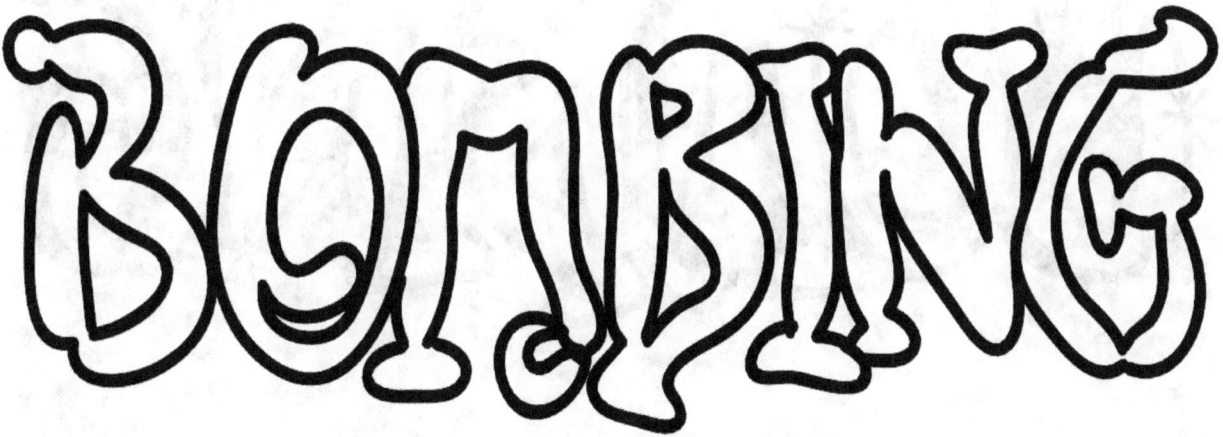

STEP 5

Shade the right side edges of the letters giving a 3D effect

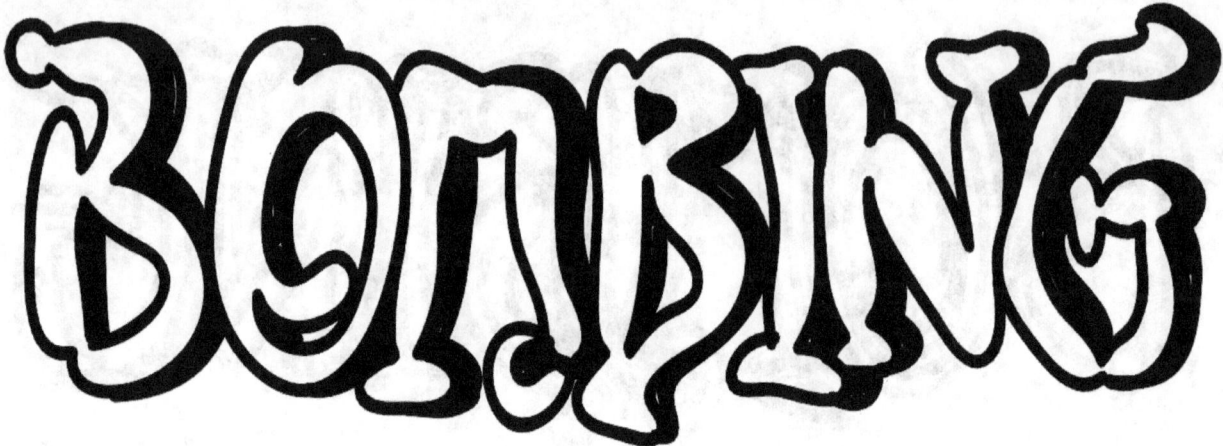

STEP 6

Add some lines that simulate a shining effect around letters with a fine stroke

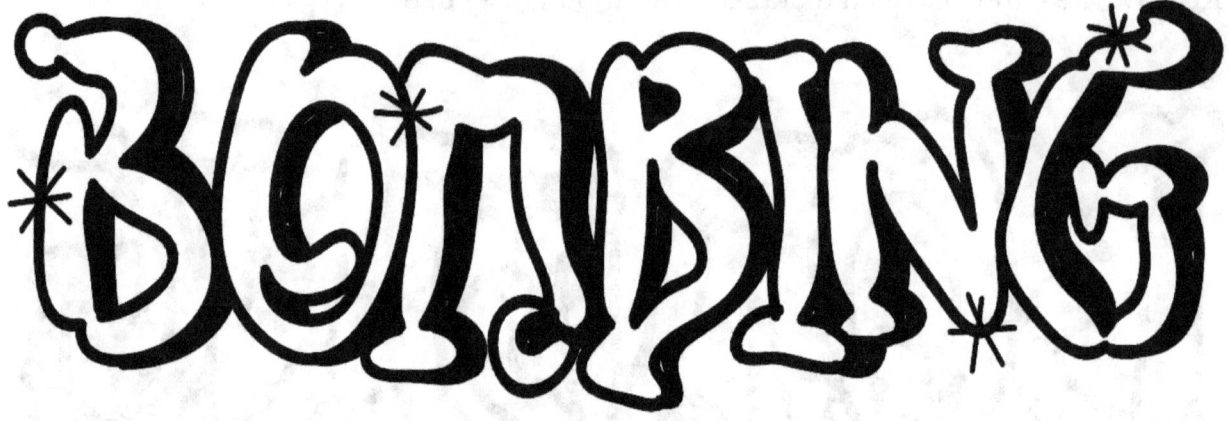

Burners:

A piece that is very well executed, typically the quality and style of art is catching

how to DRAW a BUBBLE GRAFFITI

STEP 1

Draw the word BURNERS with upper and lower case letters

BURNeRS

STEP 2

Draw around the outside and inside edges around the letters

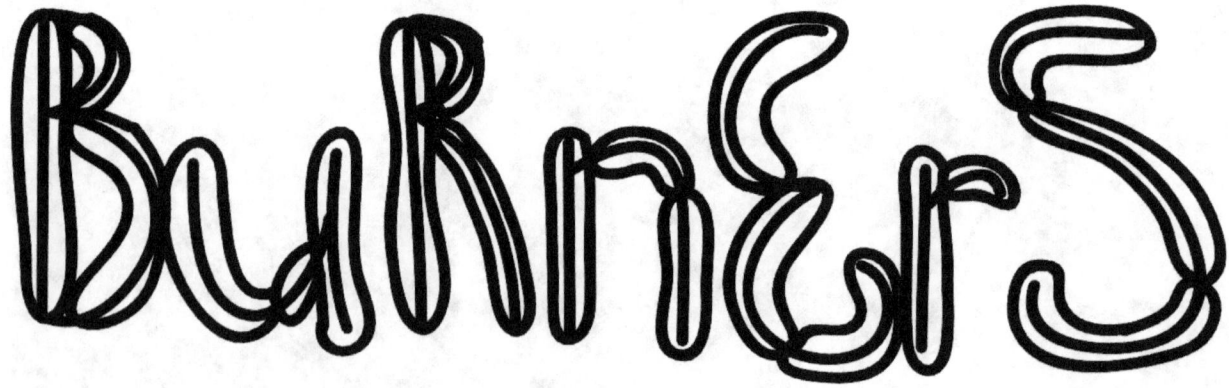

STEP 3

Redraw the letters close in distance and erase the original inside lines

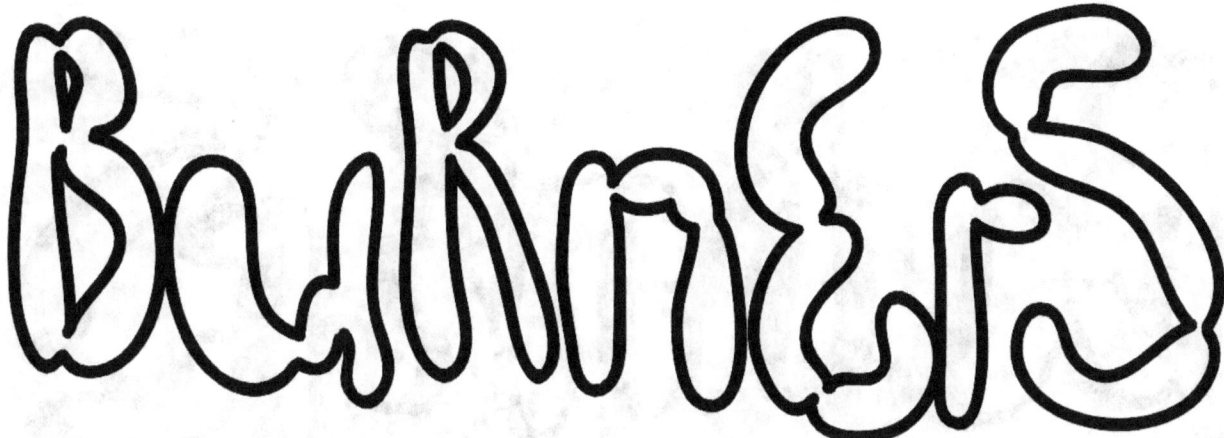

STEP 4

Add lines by dividing the letters

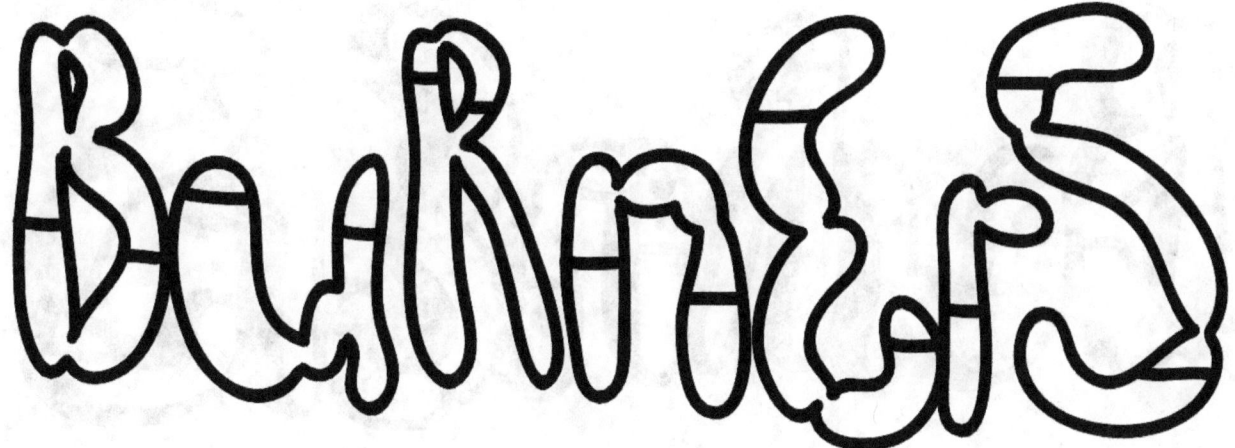

STEP 5

Shade the right side edges of the letters giving a 3D effect

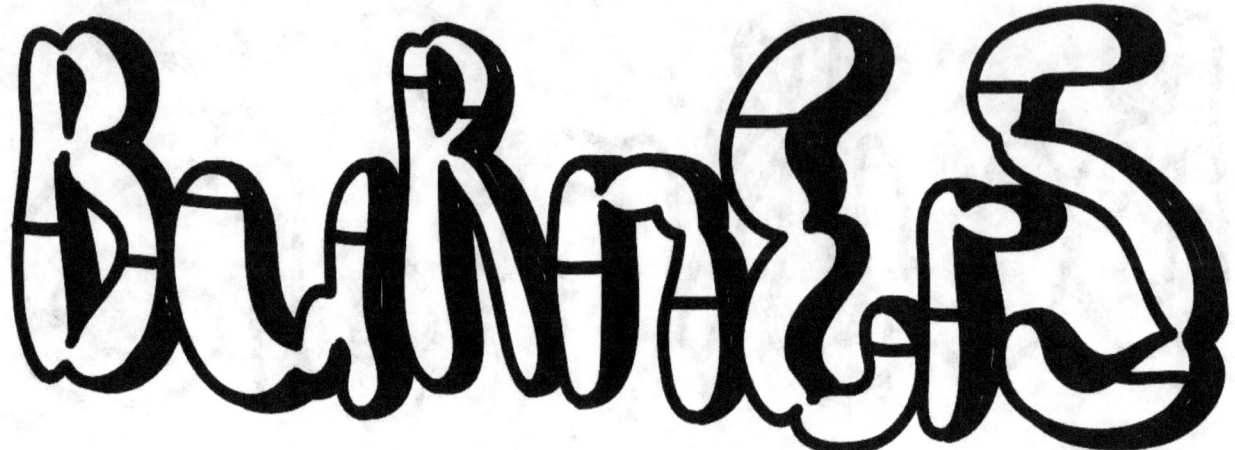

STEP 6

Add in big and tiny dots for additional letter effect

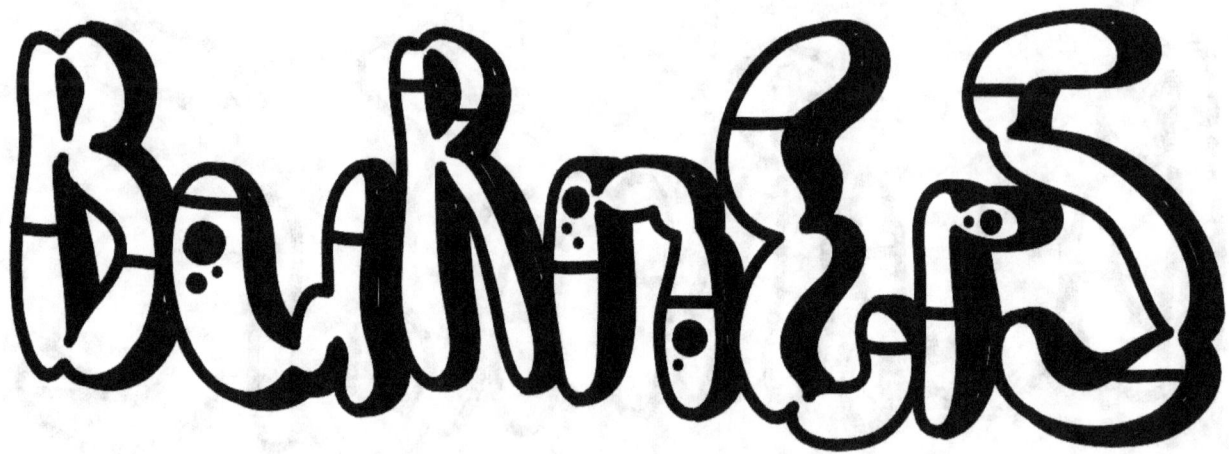

Cap:

Having two meanings when used in the graffiti world cap can be referred to the crossing out of another piece made by another artist or referred to the nozzle of a paint can

how to DRAW a BUBBLE GRAFFITI

STEP 1

Draw the word CAP

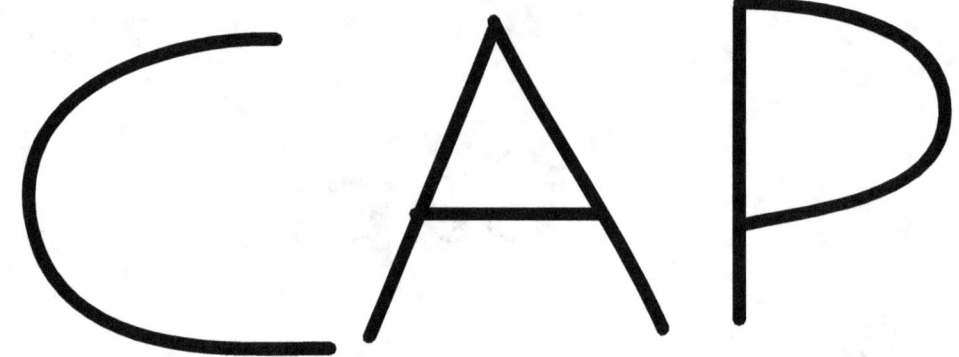

STEP 2

Draw around the outside and inside edges around the letters and erase original inner lines

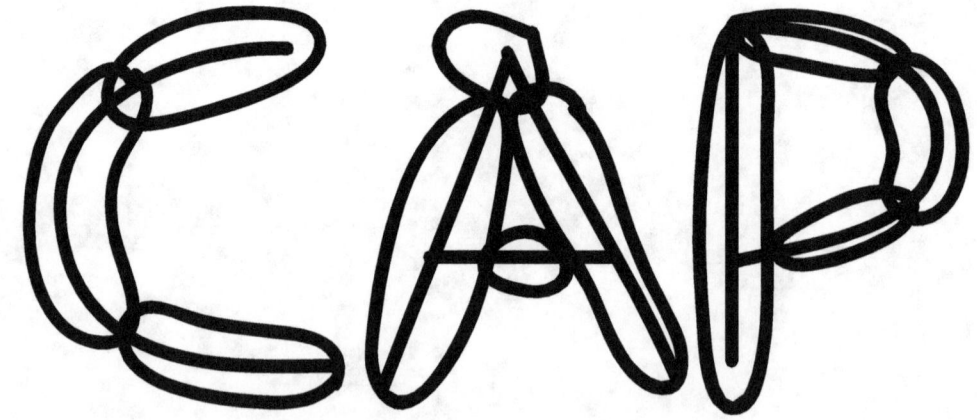

STEP 3

Redraw the letters close in distance overlapping the edges

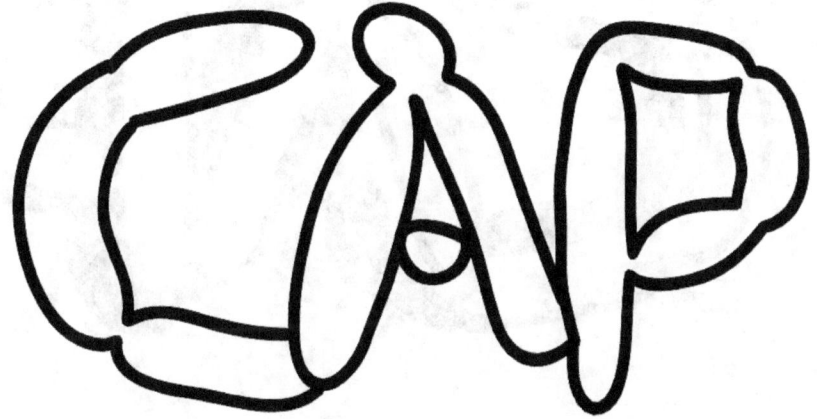

STEP 4

Add in lines with a point inside the letters near the principal lines

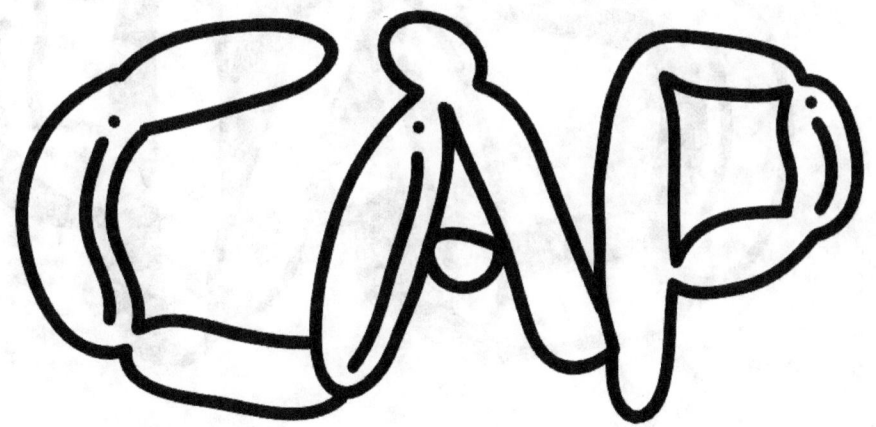

STEP 5

Shade the right side edges of the letters giving a 3D effect

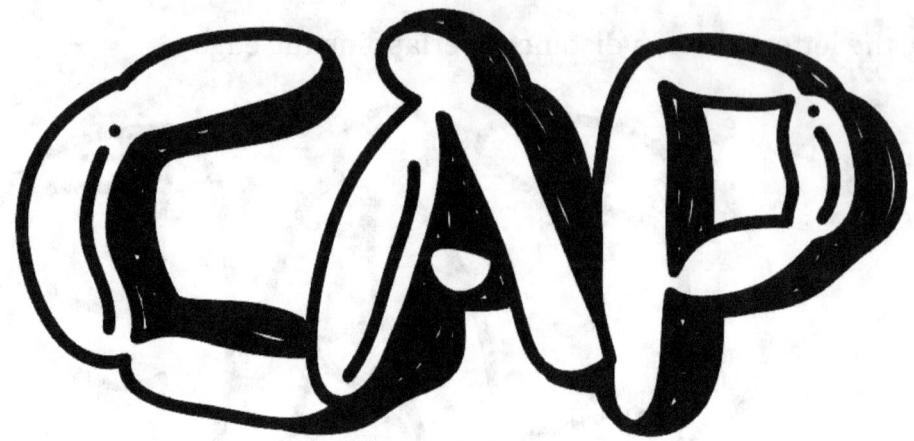

STEP 6

Add in big and tiny dots for additional letter effect

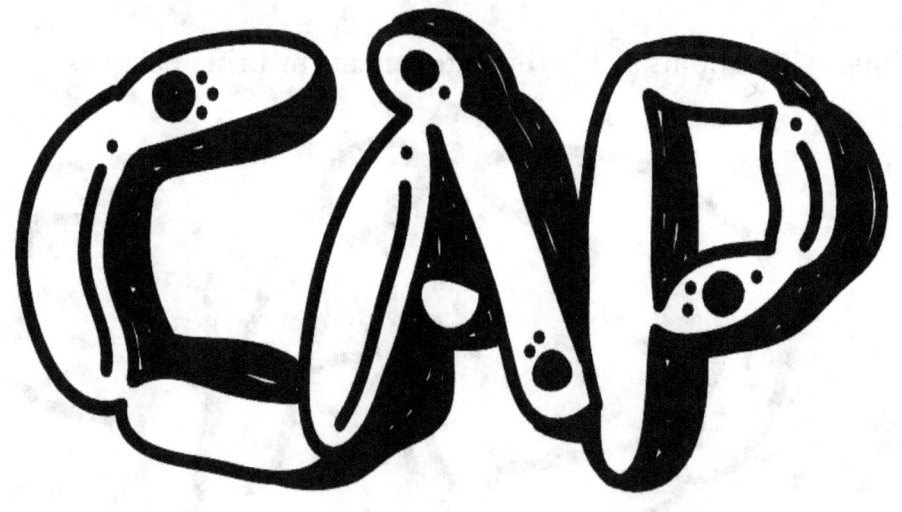

Crews:

When you are working alongside another graffiti artist together you form a crew

how to DRAW a BUBBLE GRAFFITI

STEP 1

Draw the word CREWS

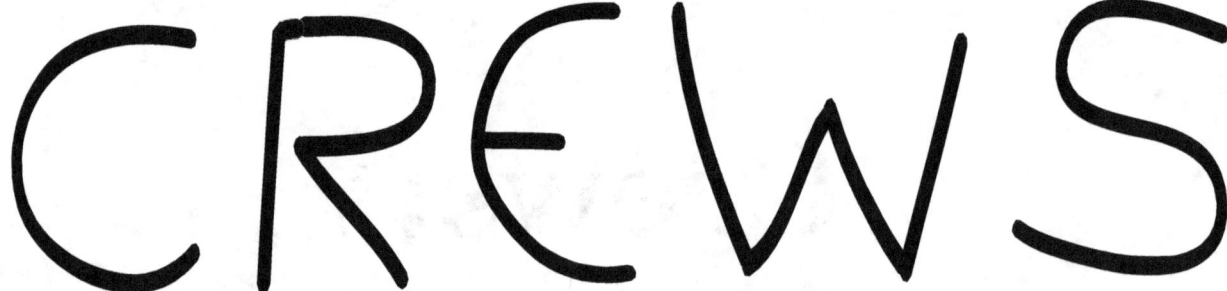

STEP 2

Now draw an outline around the letters with the size you want

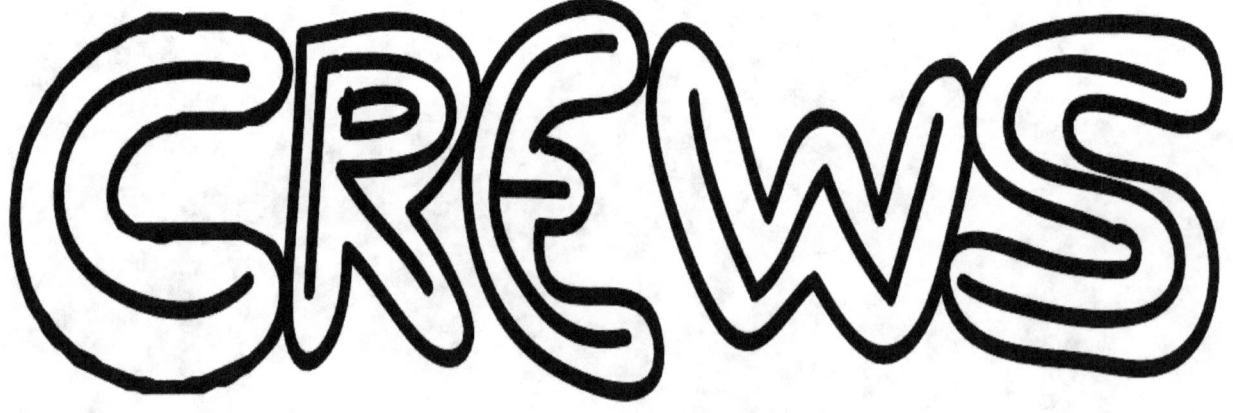

STEP 3

Redraw the word adding circles in the letters and erasing the lines in the interior

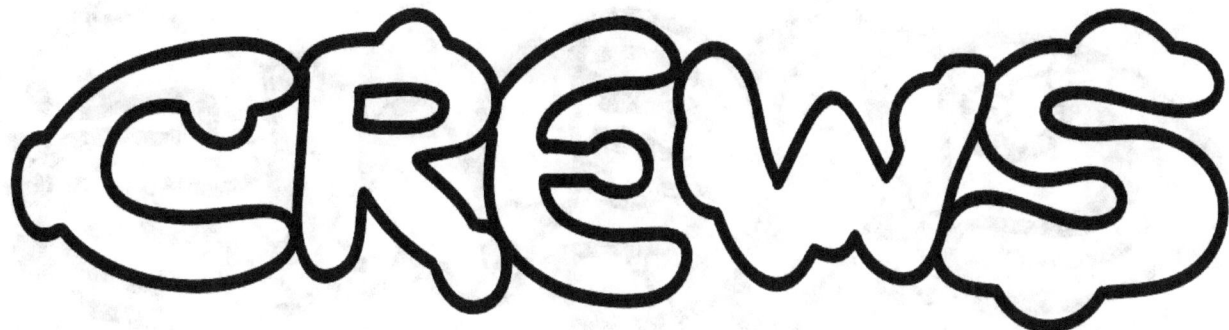

STEP 4

Add some lines with a point inside the letters near the principal lines

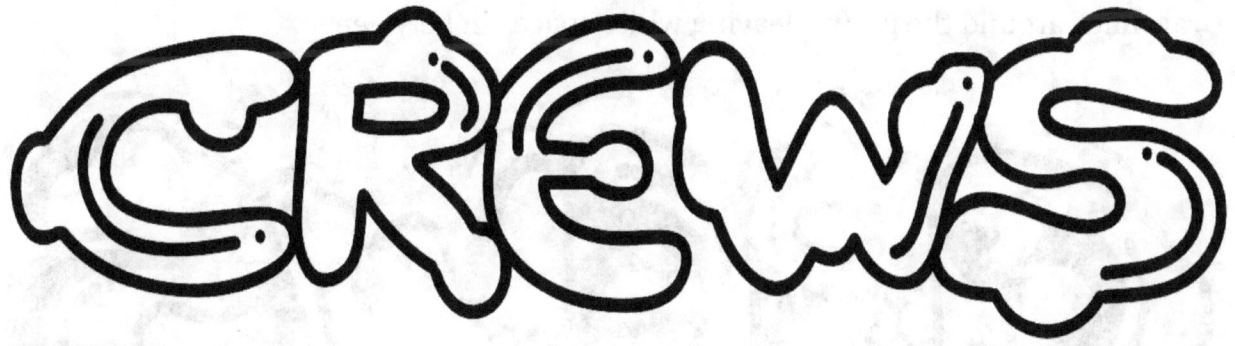

STEP 5

Shade the right side edges of the letters giving a 3D effect

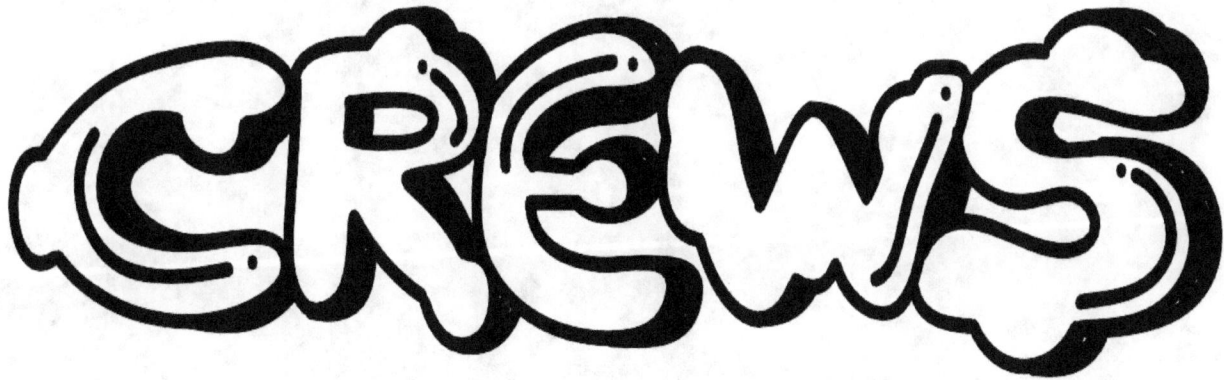

STEP 6

Add some lines with a fine stroke simulating breaks

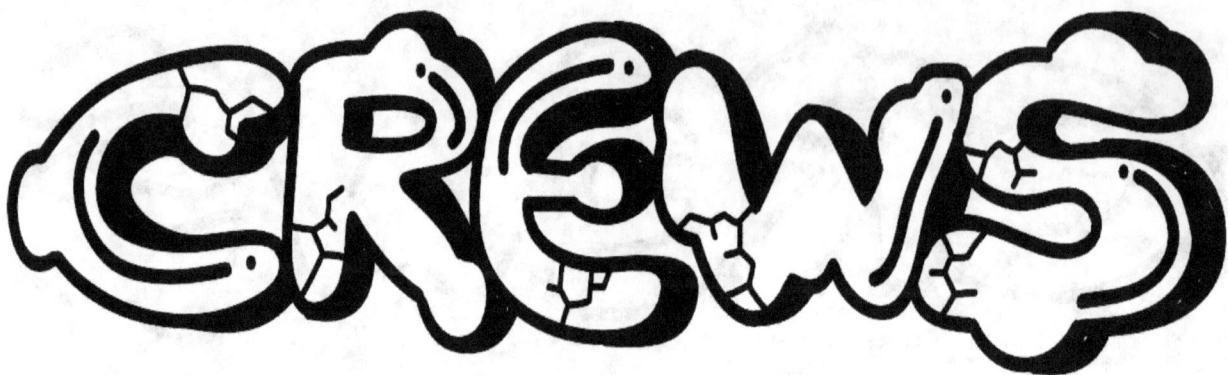

STEP 7

Draw lines around the graffiti leaving white spaces in between

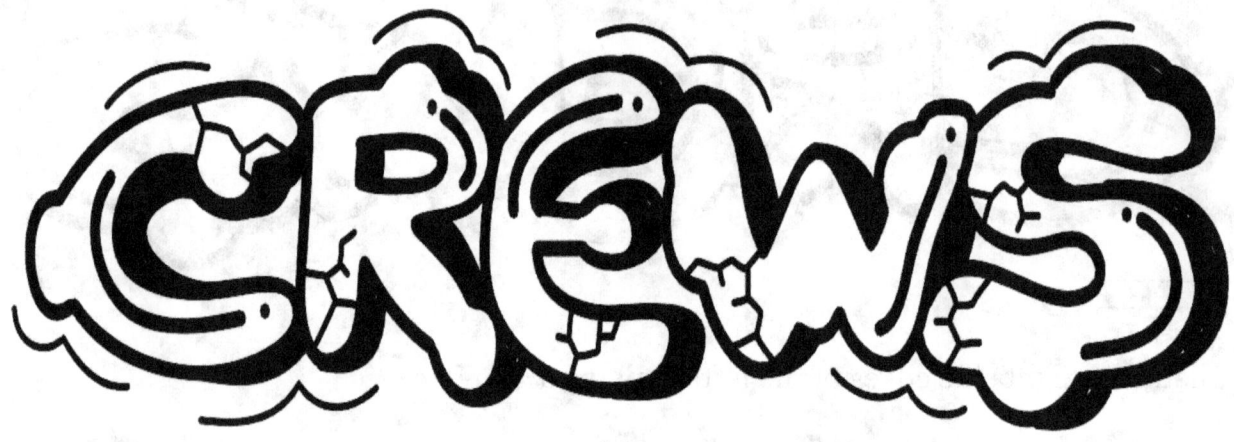

Ghost:

When paint or ink is buffed unsuccessfully, there is a left over mark known as a ghost

how to DRAW a BUBBLE GRAFFITI

STEP 1

Draw the word GHOST. Instead of the O we will draw a "pacman"

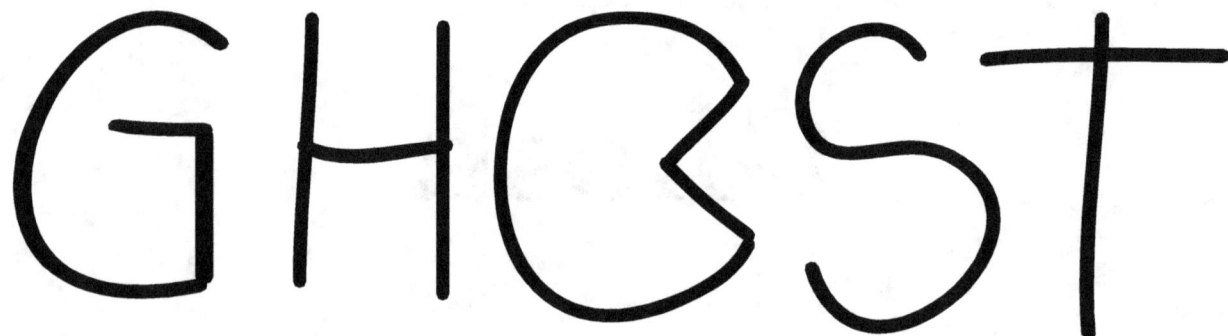

STEP 2

Now draw an outline around the letters with the size you want, but not in the "pacman"

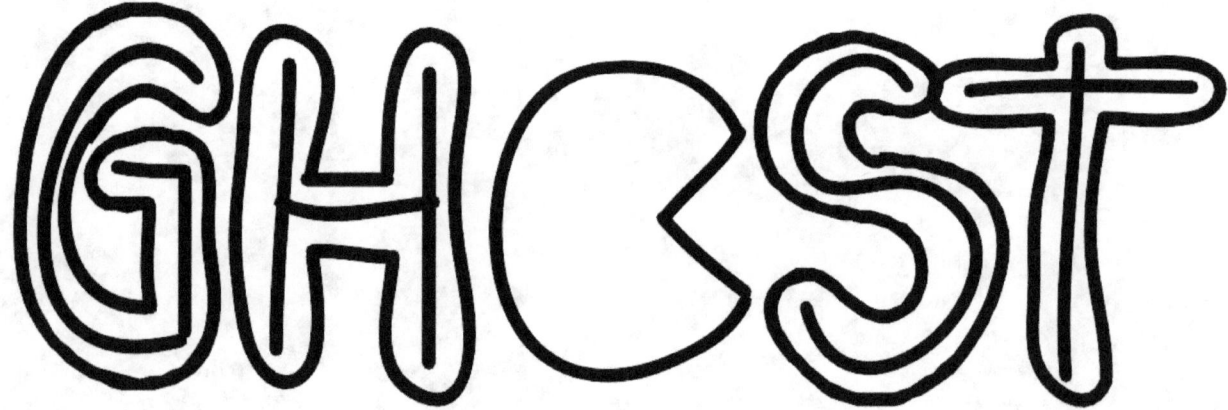

STEP 3

Redraw the letters close in distance and erase the original inside lines

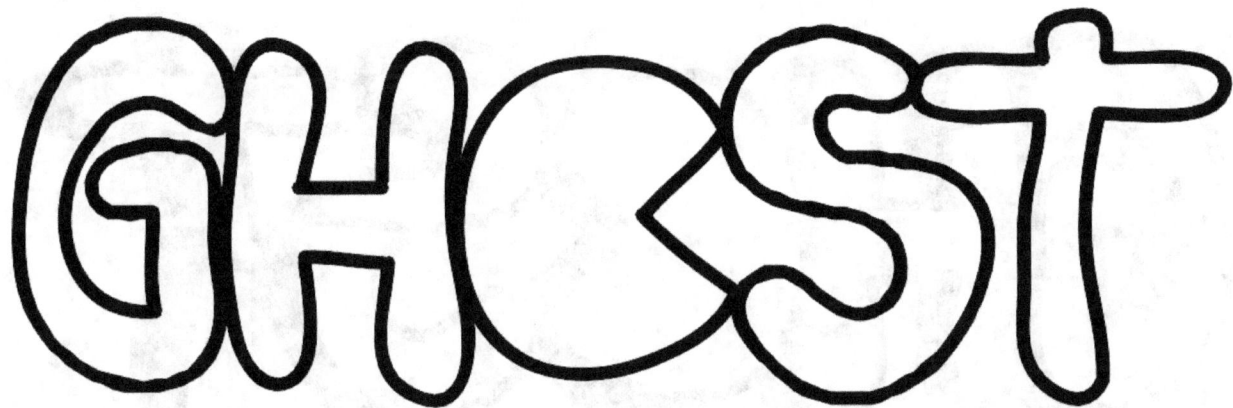

STEP 4

Add some lines crossing the letters, preferably in the middle

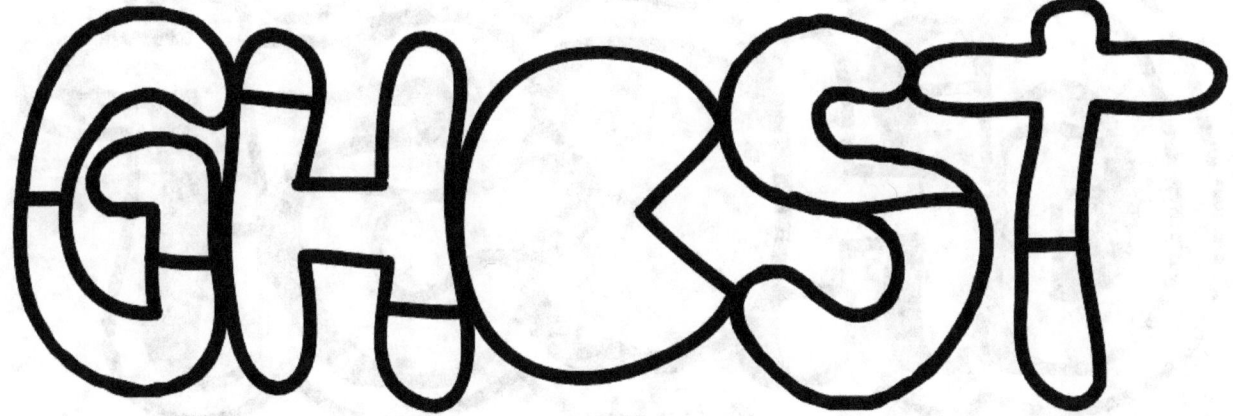

STEP5

Shade the right side edges of the letters giving a 3D effect

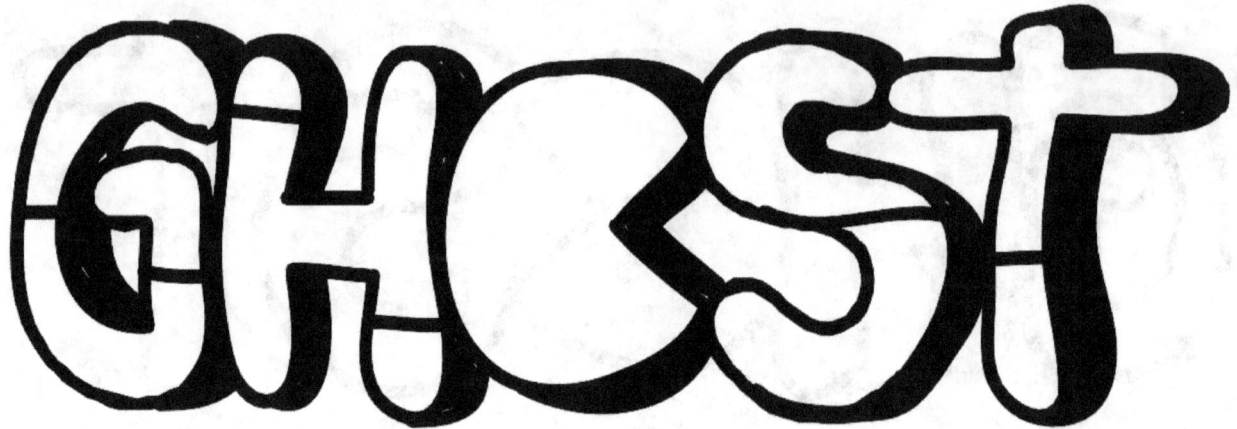

STEP6

Draw a line around the graffiti with a fine continuous stroke

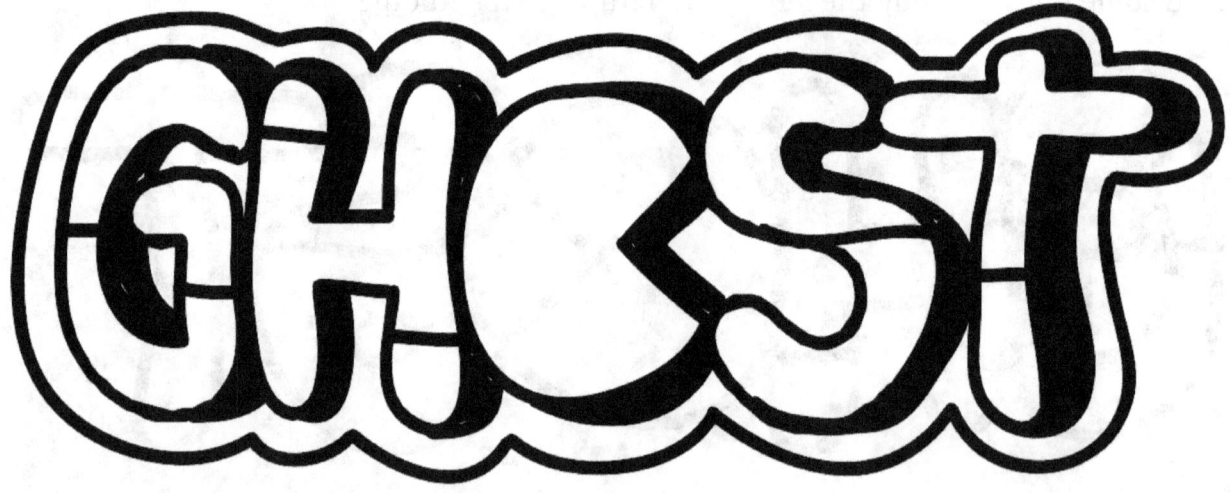

Stickers:

As mentioned previously, stickers are prepared before they are applied to material object

how to DRAW a BUBBLE GRAFFITI

STEP 1

Draw the word STICKERS

STICKERS

STEP 2

Now draw an outline around the letters with the size you want

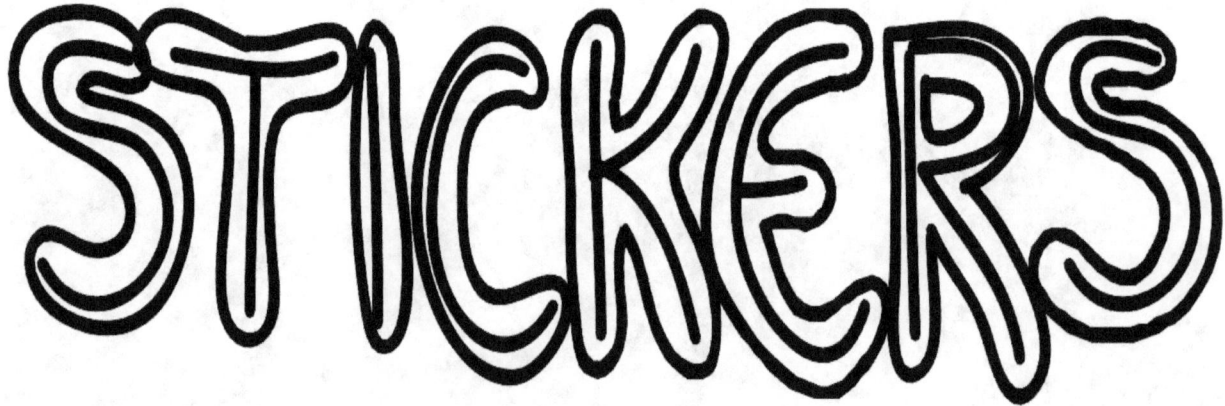

STEP 3

Redraw the word adding circles in the extremes and erasing the lines in the interior

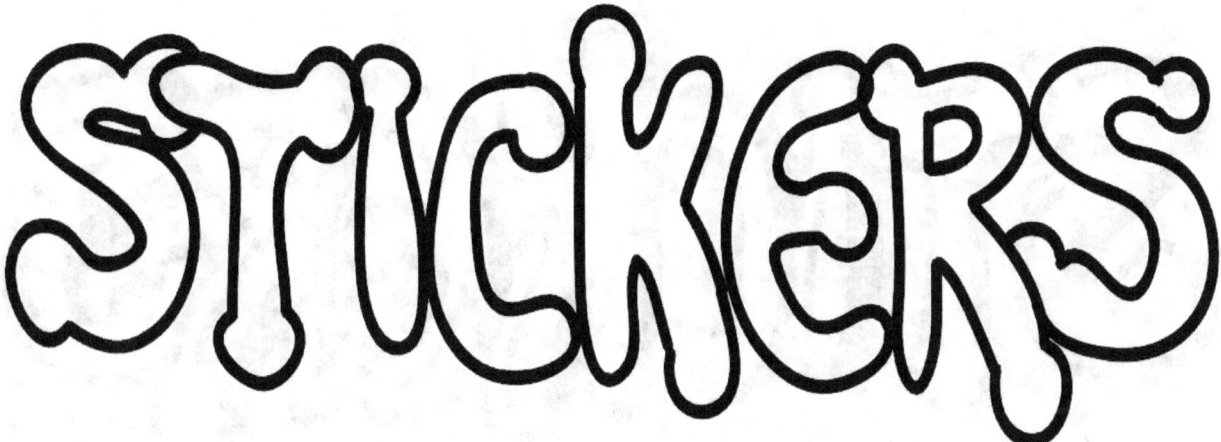

STEP 4

Add some lines with a point inside the letters near the principal lines

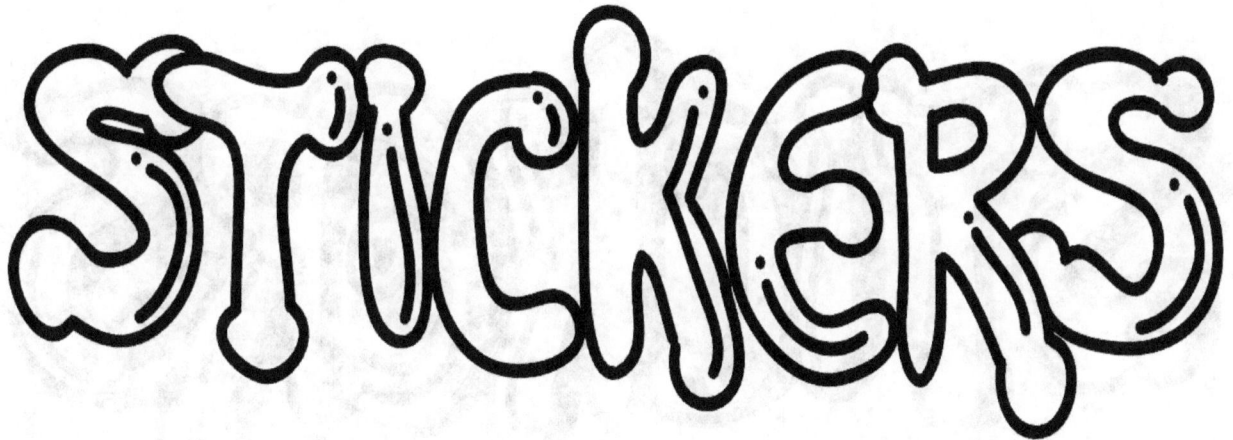

STEP 5

Shade the right-side edges of the letters giving a 3D effect

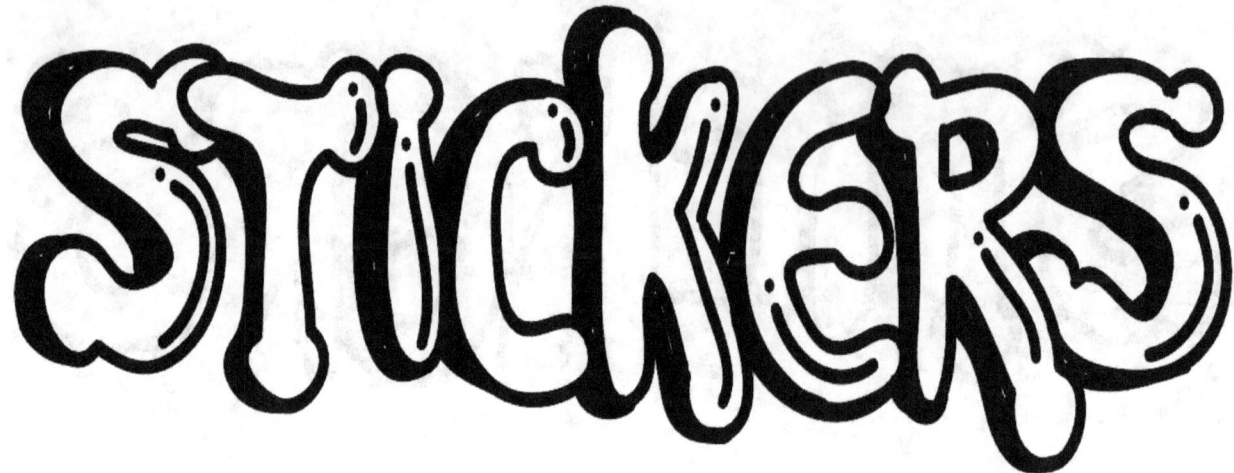

STEP 6

Add filled in triangles for additional letter effect

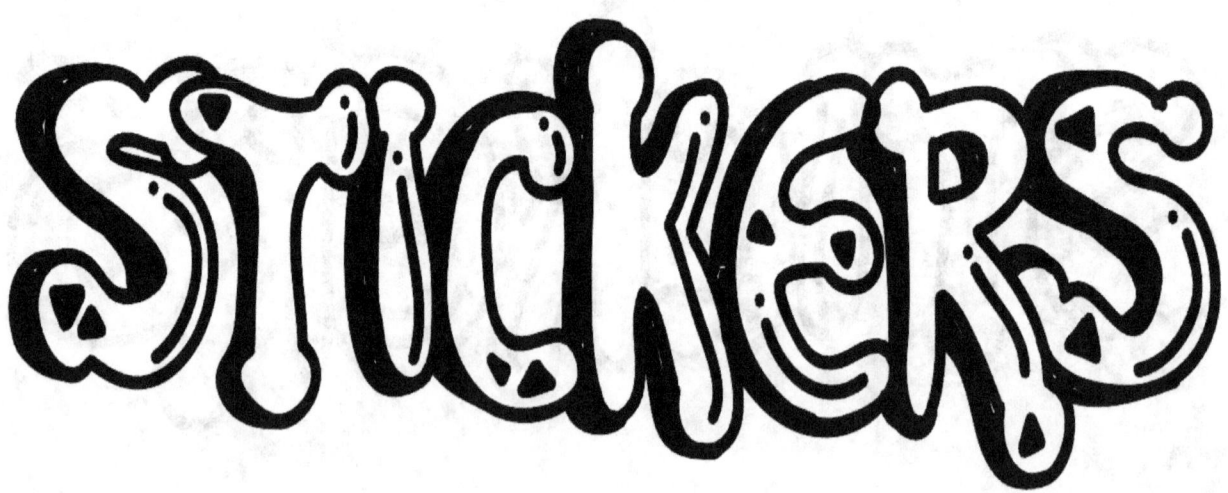

How to Draw a Freestyle Graffiti/ Creative Piecing

Blade:

Blade also known as The King of Graffiti. Blade is best remembered for his iconic character imagery work on whole cars and paintings on over 5,000 trains

how to DRAW a FREESTYLE GRAFFITI

STEP 1

Draw the name BLADE

BLADE

STEP 2

Draw fine outlines around the letters, making them round and bubbly ignoring the inner part

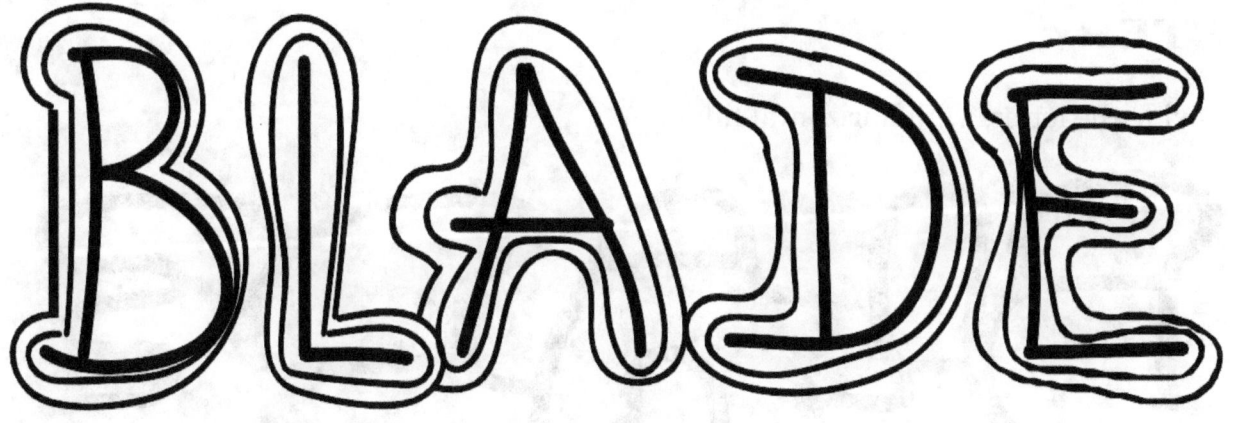

STEP 3

Draw the letters again using only the outside line

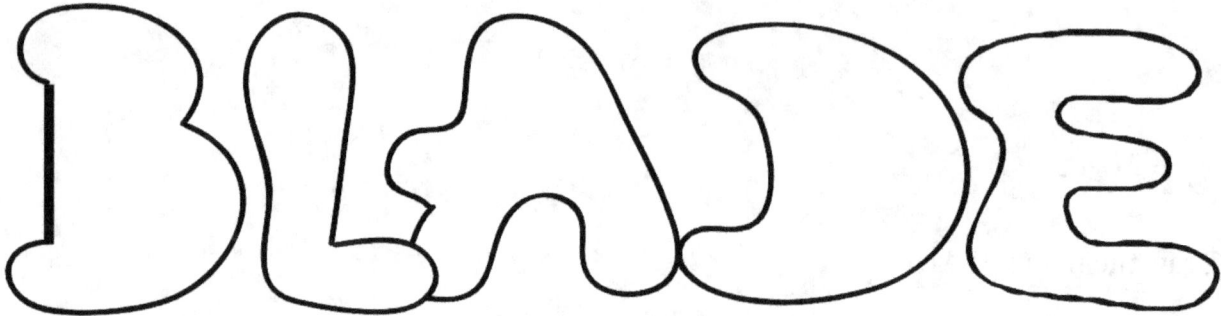

STEP 4

Redraw the letters close together, overlapping them just a little

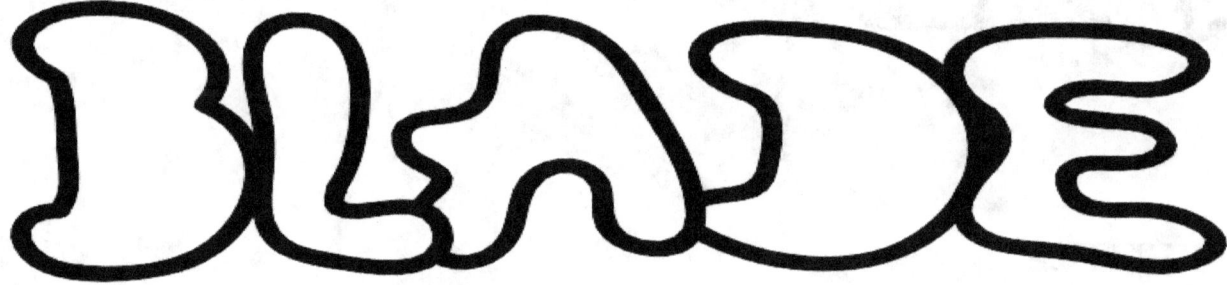

STEP 5

Divide the letters with horizontal lines

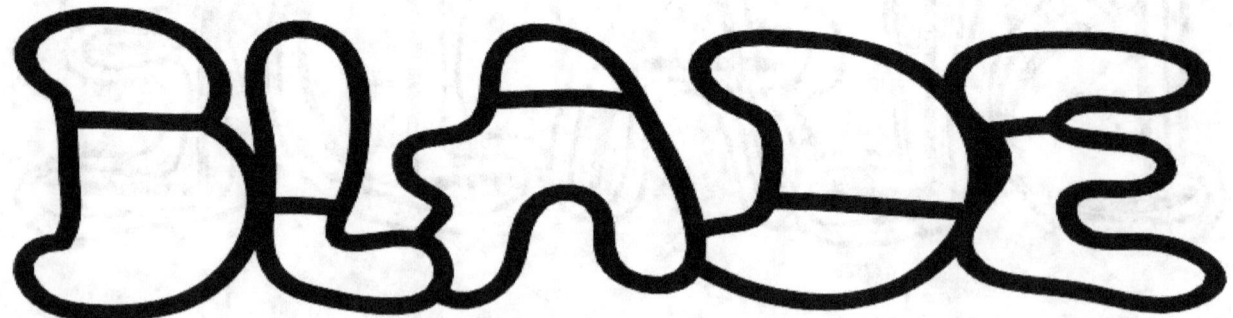

STEP 6

Fill with black alternateparts

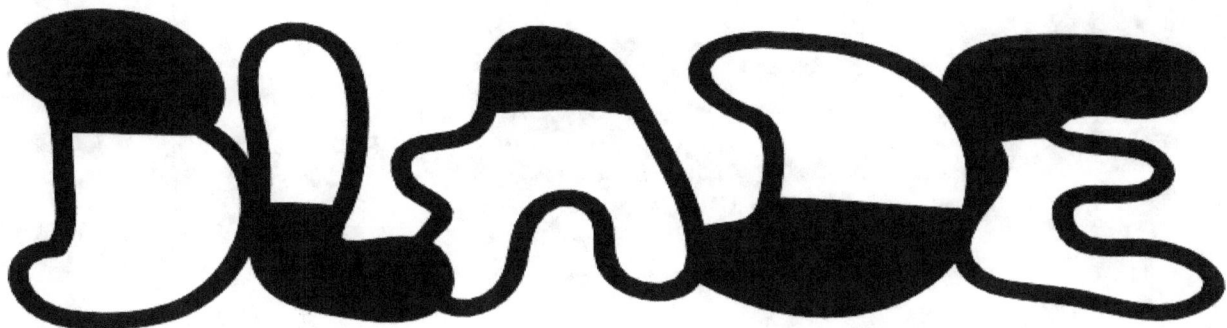

STEP 7

Draw internal black lines on the white part and white lines on the black part, following a continuity. All lines with a extra fine stroke

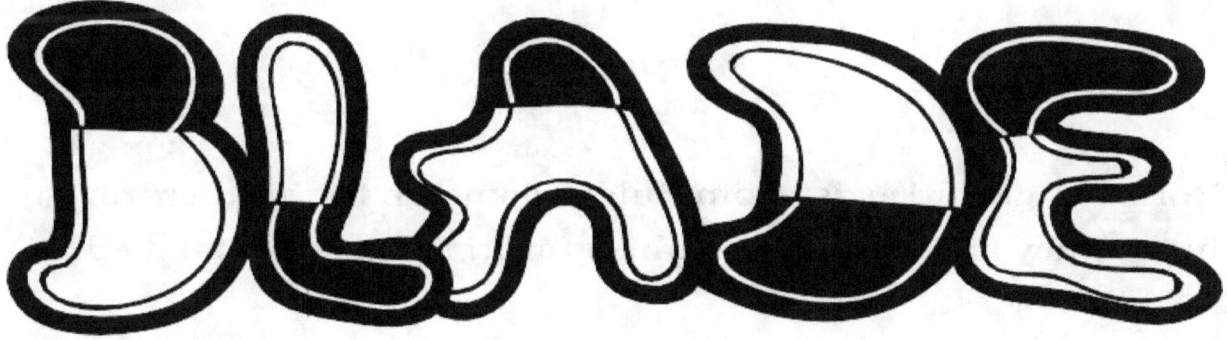

STEP 8

Add curves around the background to give tag more attraction

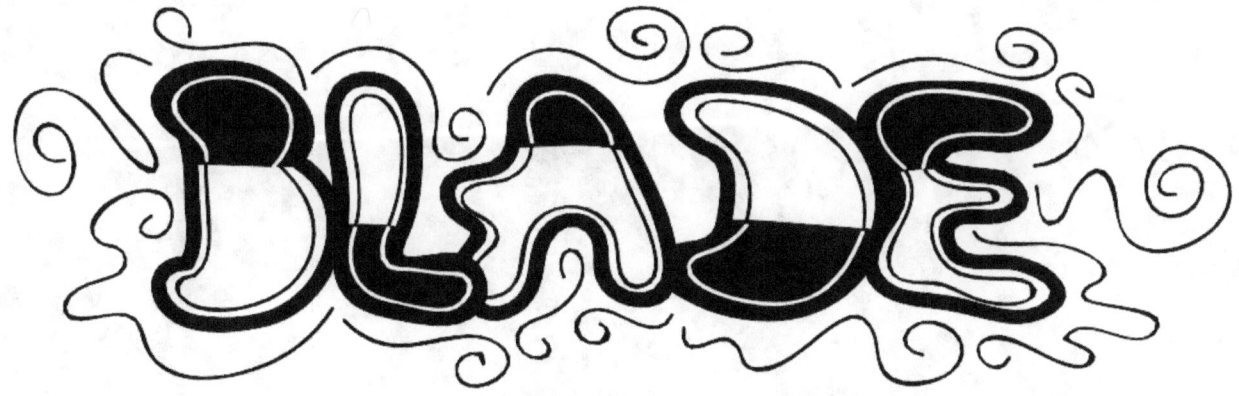

Boris:

Boris is a graffiti artist from Bulgaria known for his disregard to his privacy and marketing of his graffiti through social media

how to DRAW a FREESTYLE GRAFFITI

STEP 1

Draw the name BORIS with tag style letters

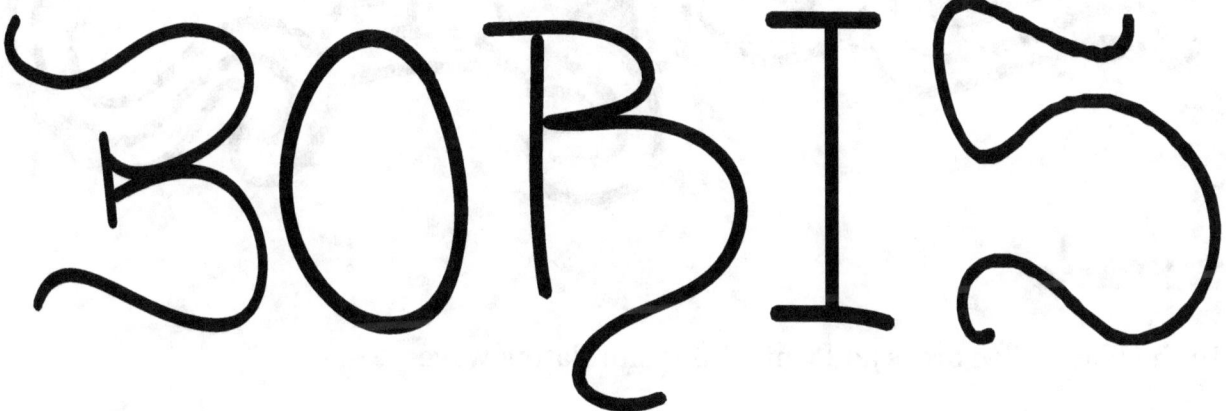

STEP 2

Draw an outline around the letters

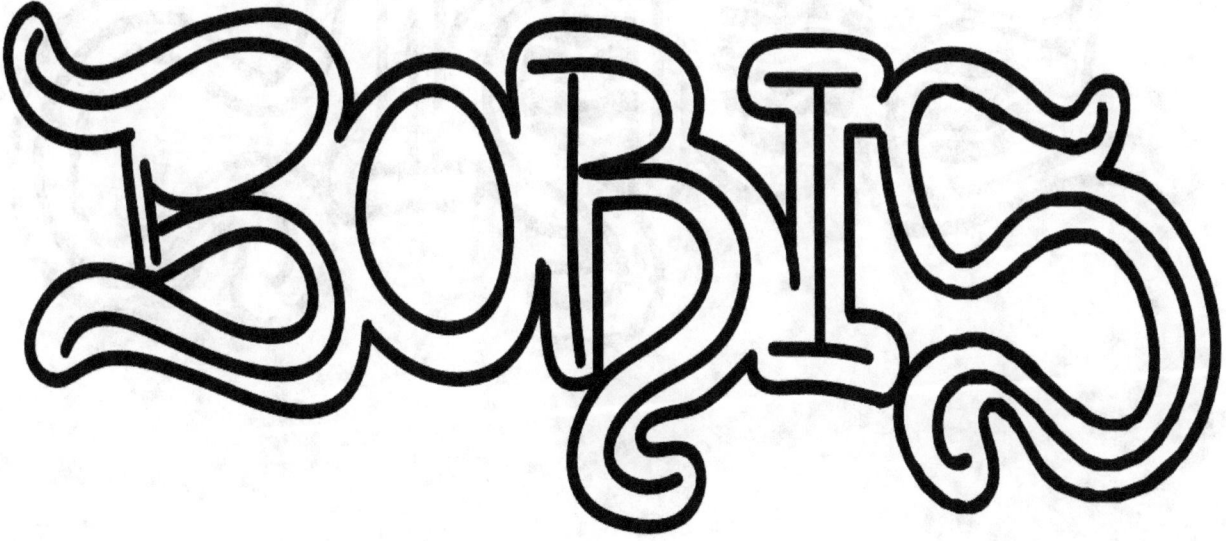

STEP 3

Fill in the parts that are closed

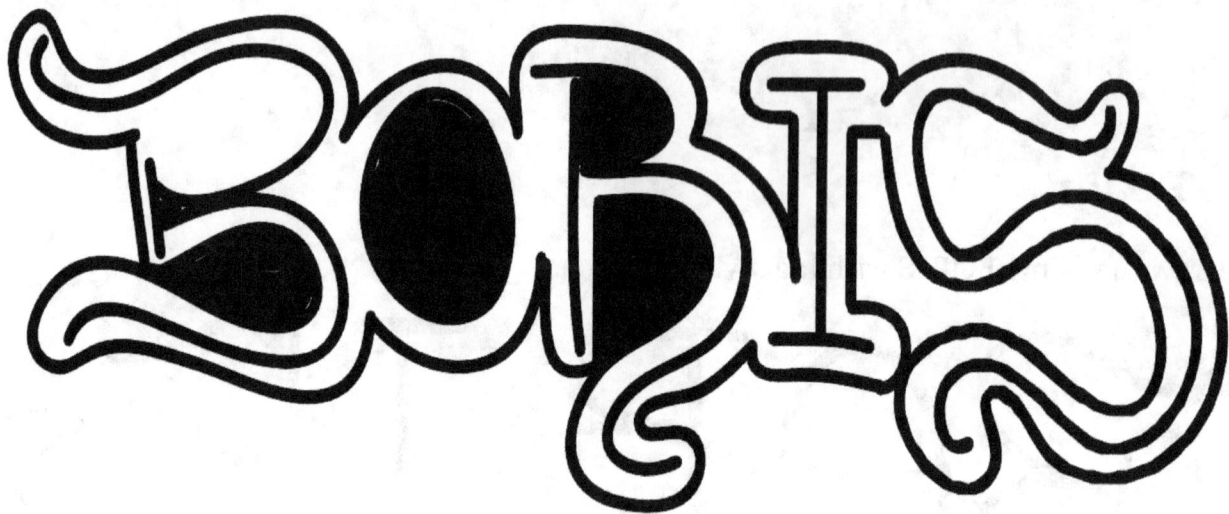

STEP 4

In the black filled areas add white lines simulating waves

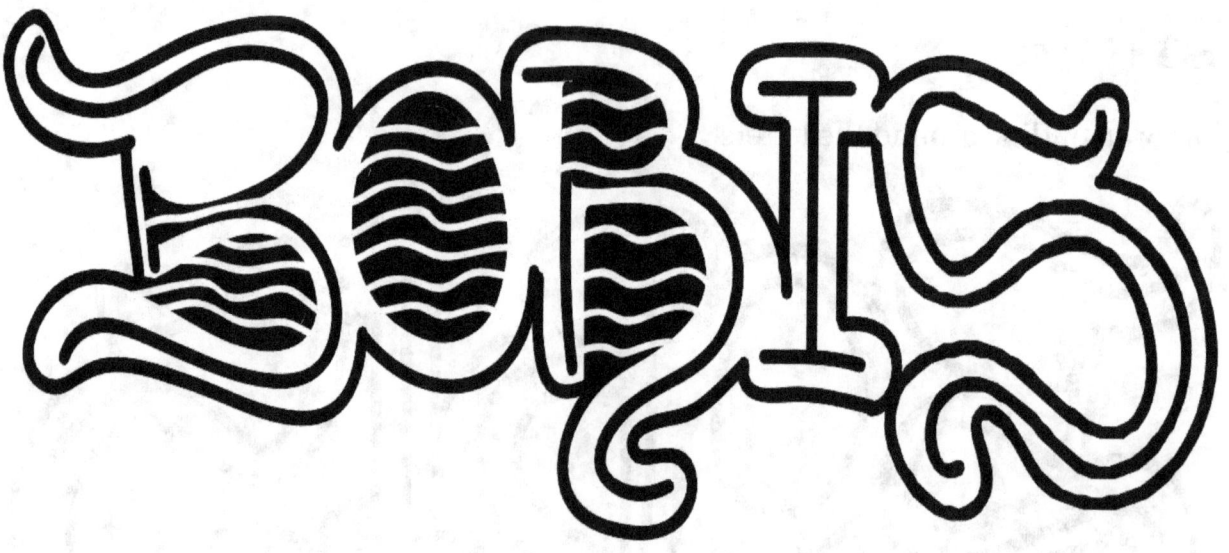

STEP 5

Shade the letters from different angles generating an irregular 3D effect

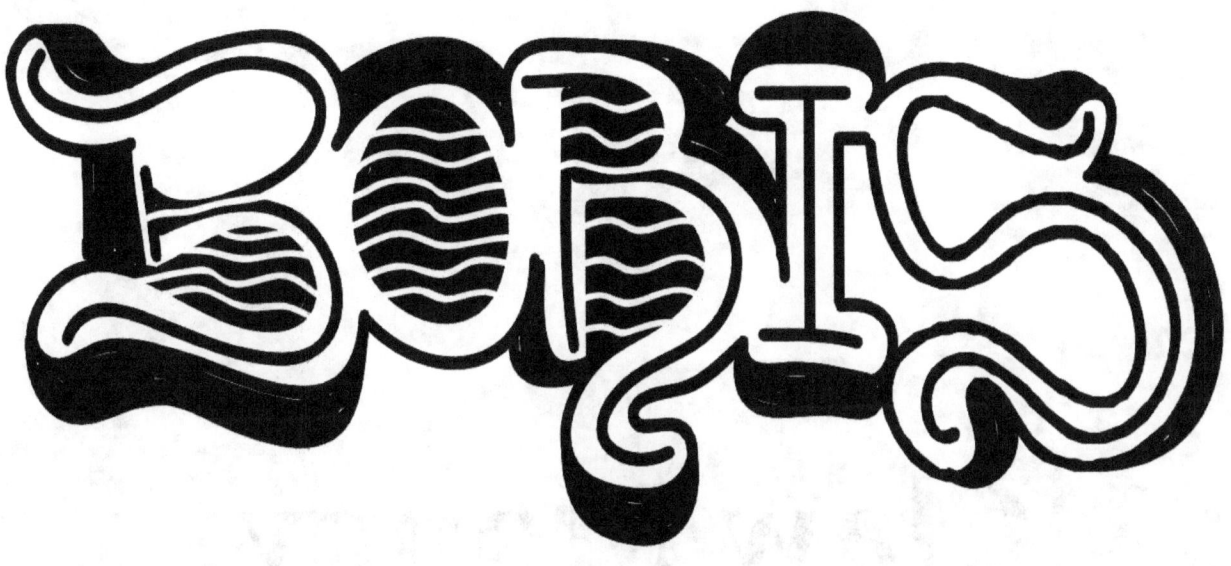

STEP 6

Add a fine outline with waveforms

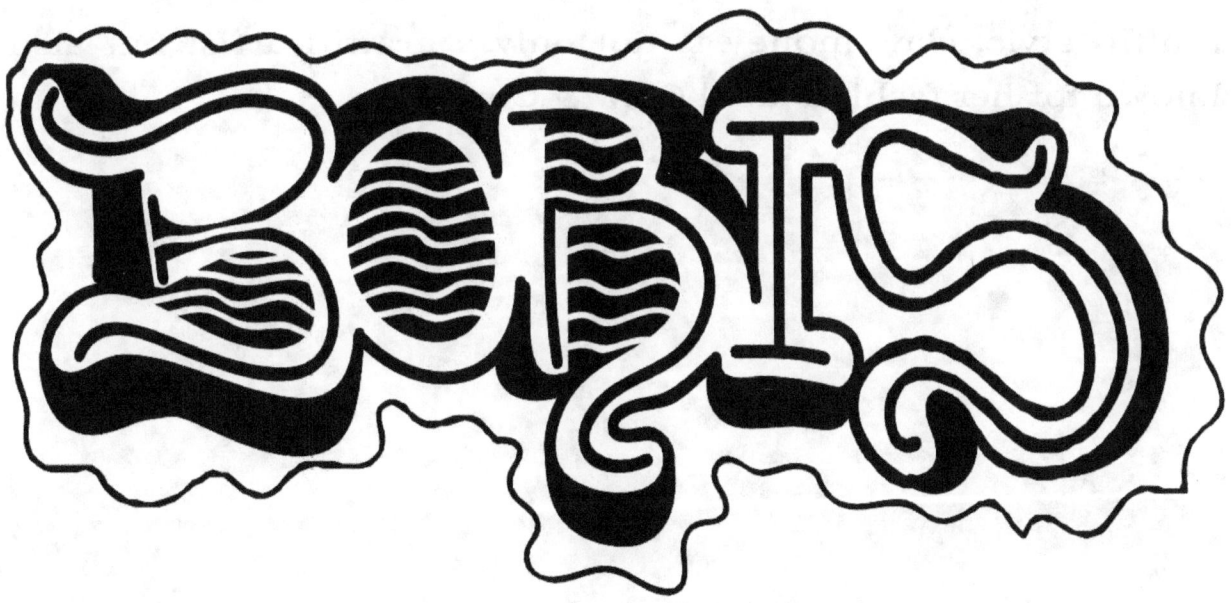

Claw Money:

Known for her iconic claw symbol that has become part of her graffiti style, claw money is not only a graffiti artist but also known for her fashion label Claw & Company

how to DRAW a FREESTYLE GRAFFITI

STEP 1

Draw in a few lines as a template

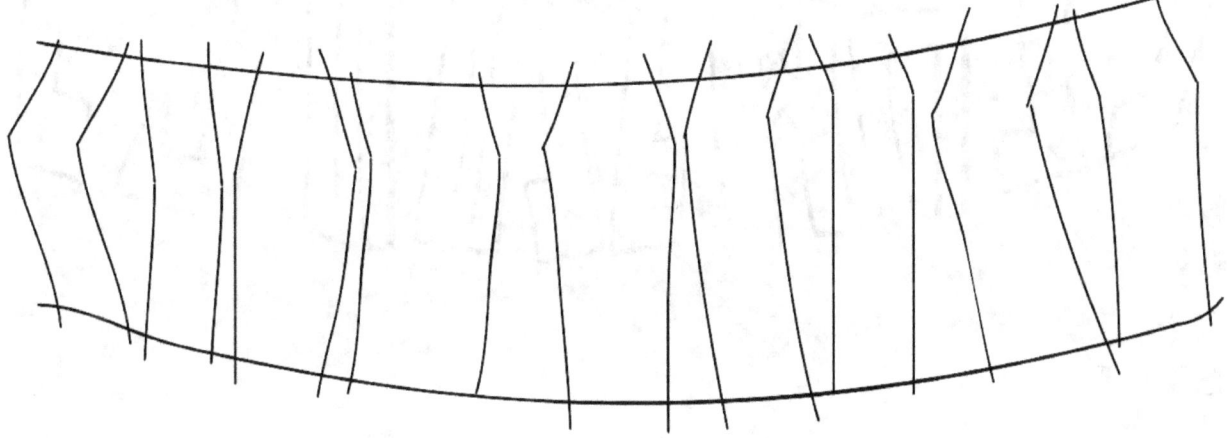

STEP 2

Draw the name CLAW MONEY following this template

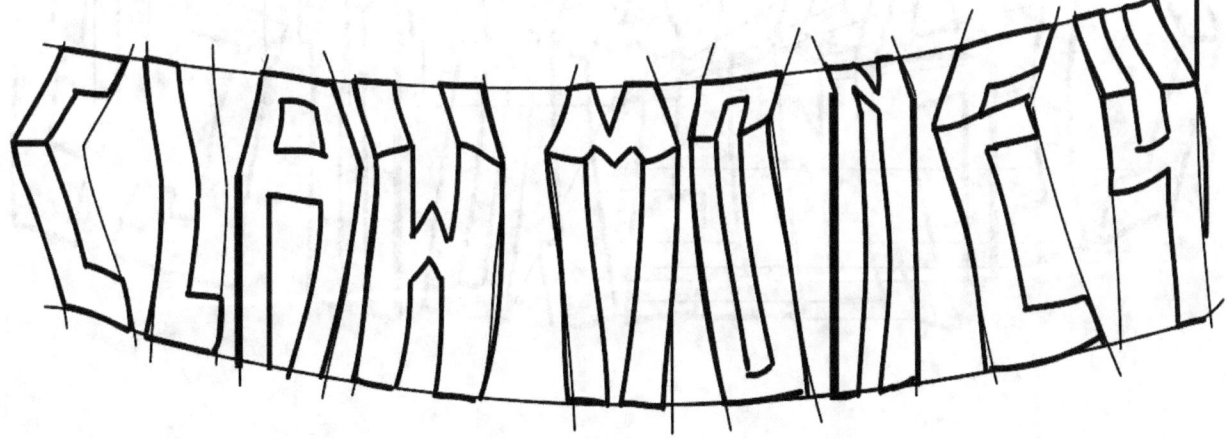

STEP 3

Erase the template and redraw the sketch to modify the letters with some decorative elements

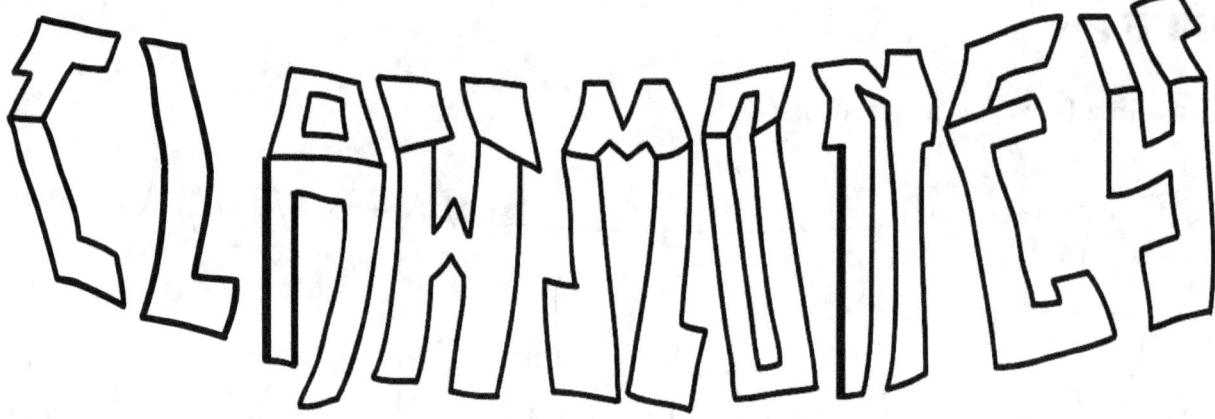

STEP 4

Add additional lines from each vertex that converge in the center of the sketch for a later 3D effect. These will be used as a template

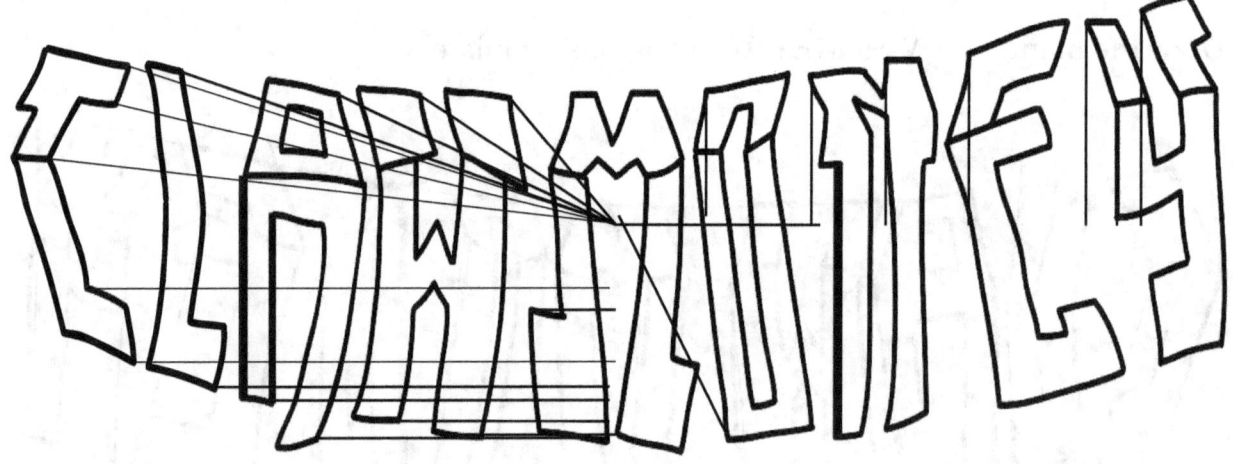

STEP 5

Redraw this sketch following lines

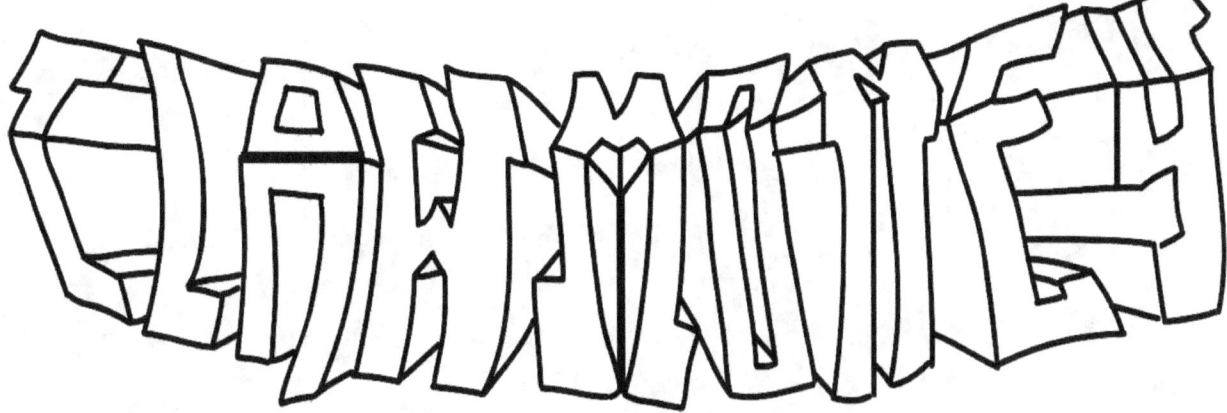

STEP 6

Draw 3D lines of different thicknesses

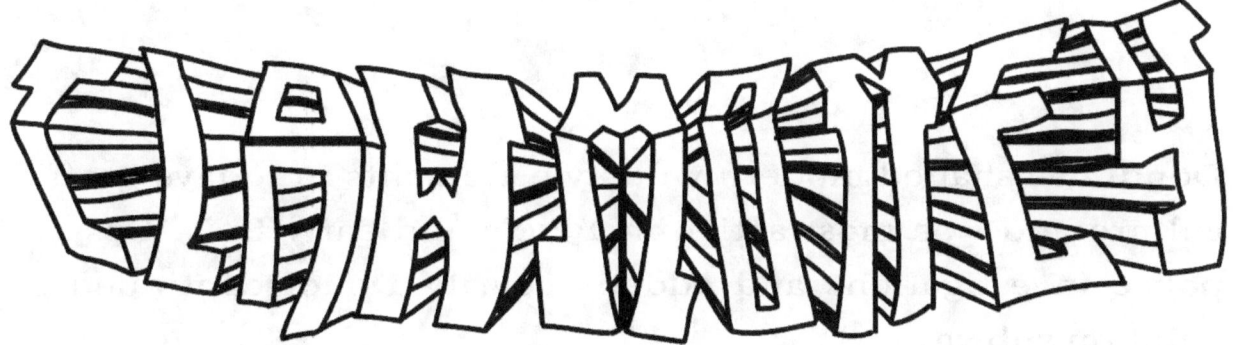

Step 7

Add in lines with small dots near the principal letter lines

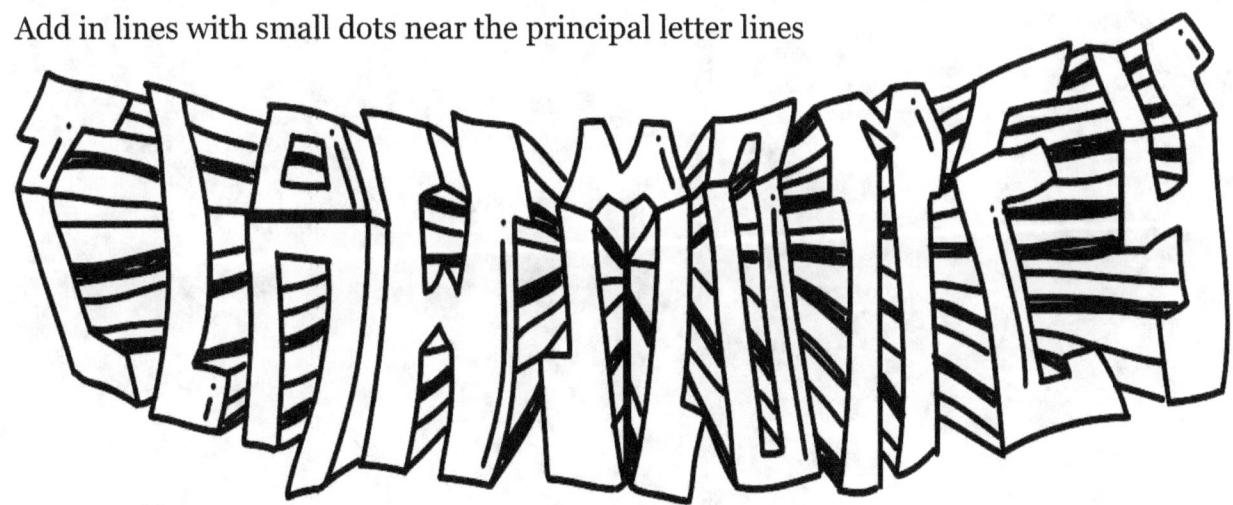

Dondi:

Dondi has shaped modern wildstyle elements in todays graffiti culture and was most active in 1970's and early 80's. Despite police investigations and added security Dondi continued to paint on subways

to DRAW a FREESTYLE GRAFFITI

STEP 1

Draw in unconnected inverted lines to use as a template for each letter of the name DONDI

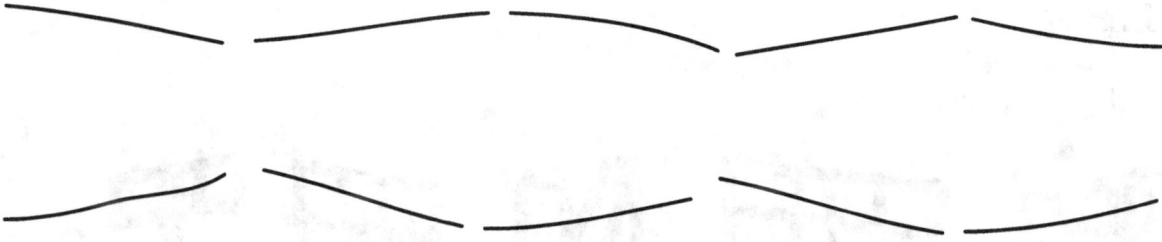

STEP 2

Draw the name DONDI with rectangular letters following the template

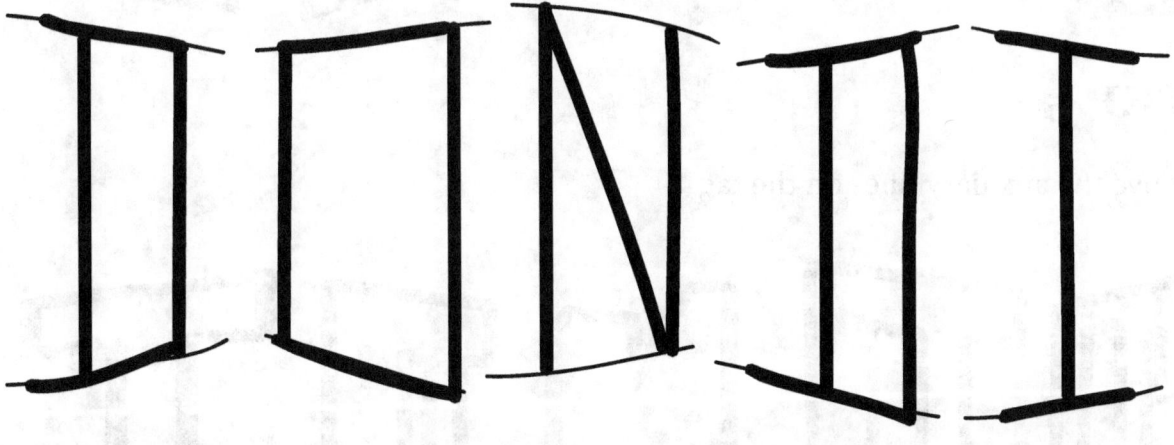

STEP 3

Delete the lines of the templates and add some details in the letters

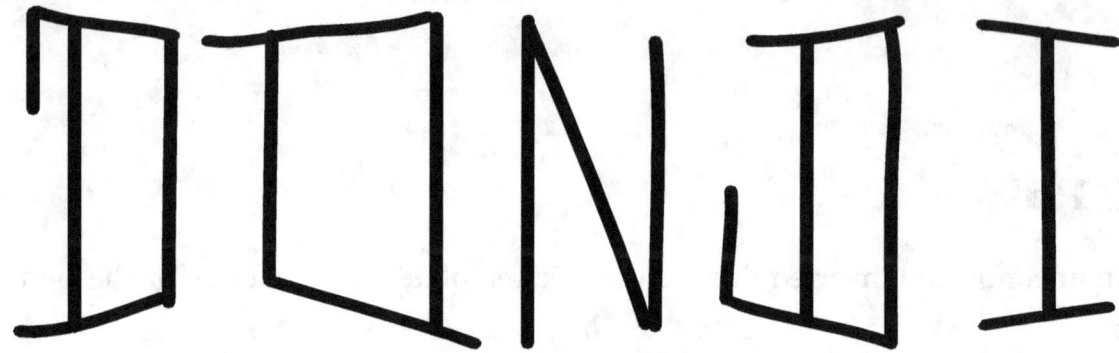

STEP 4

Add wide rectangular bars

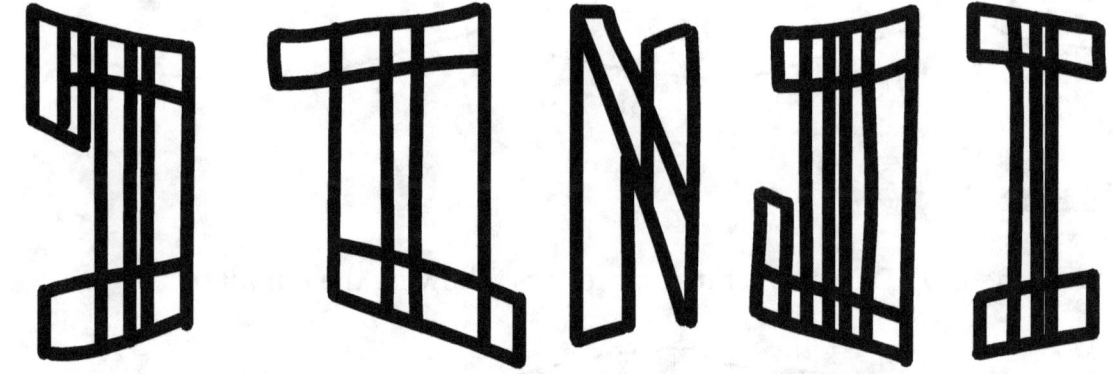

STEP 5

Remove the auxiliary lines on the tag

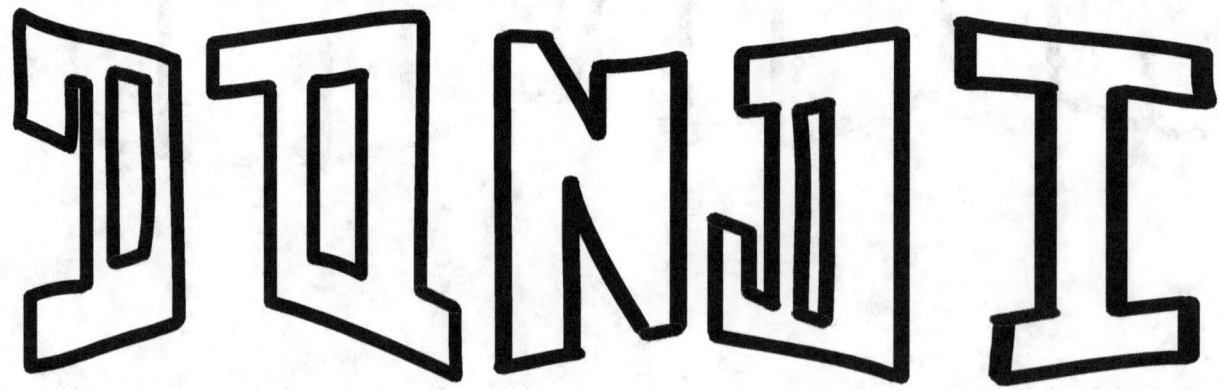

STEP 6

Shade the letters on both sides generating a 3D perspective

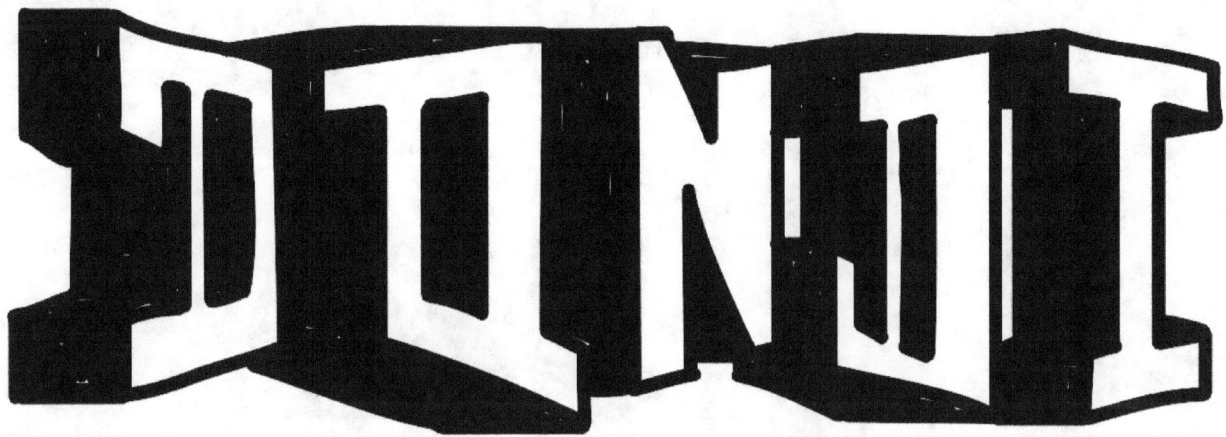

STEP 7

As a final step, make an outline around the letters with an extra thin stroke

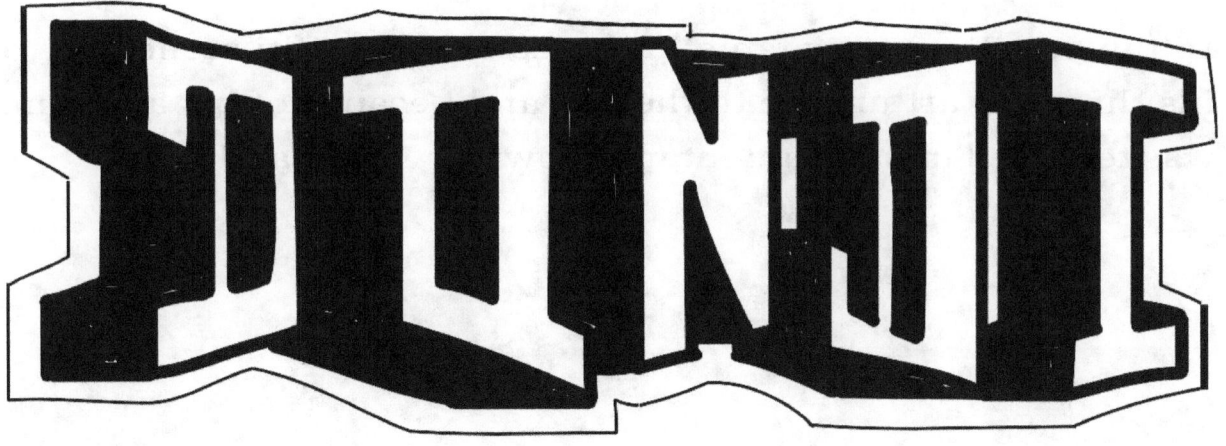

Eine:

In the 90's Eine grew fame in the London Graffiti scene due to his throw up art unique to the city and because of his art, Eine was televised in a documentary known as Kinds and Toys.

how to DRAW a FREESTYLE GRAFFITI

STEP 1

Draw the name EINE with a manuscript style

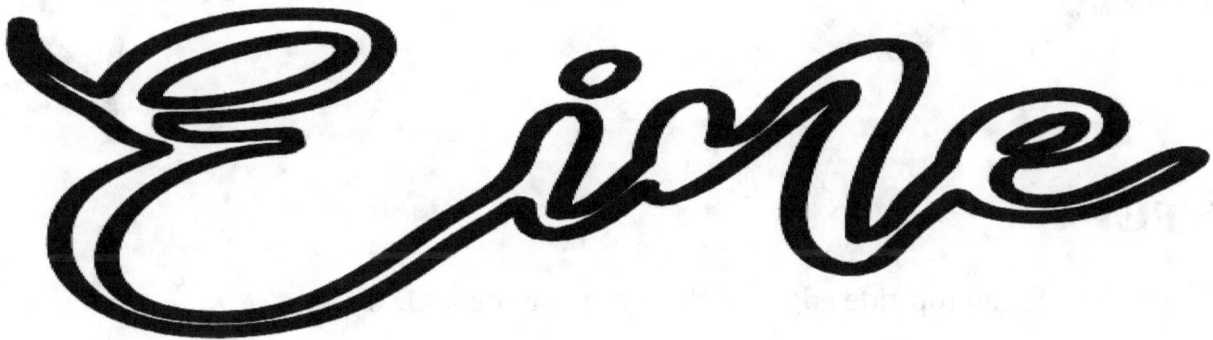

STEP 2

Add decorative elements to these letters

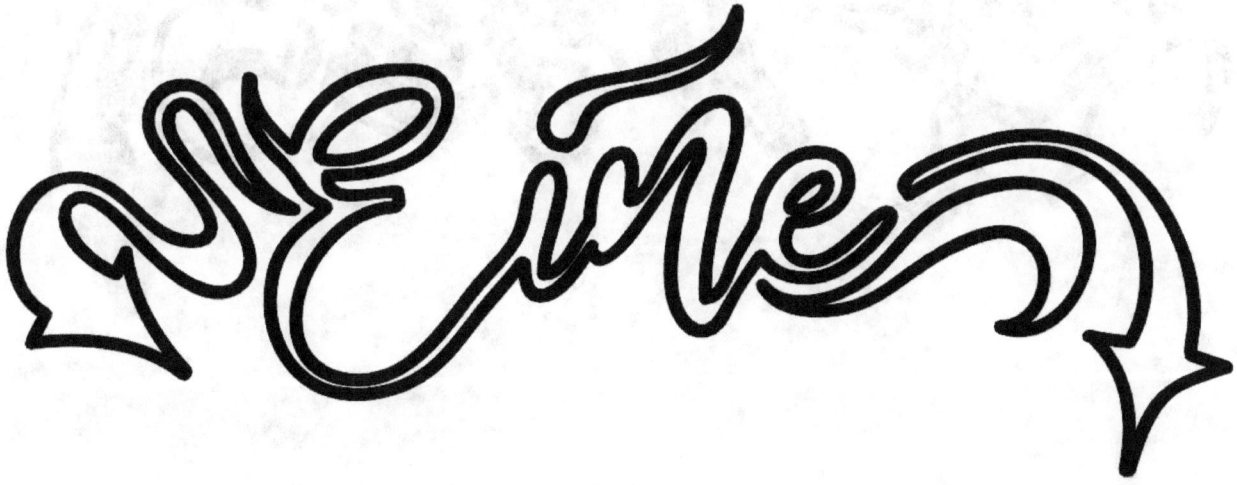

STEP 3

Cut part of some letters and arrows in bits

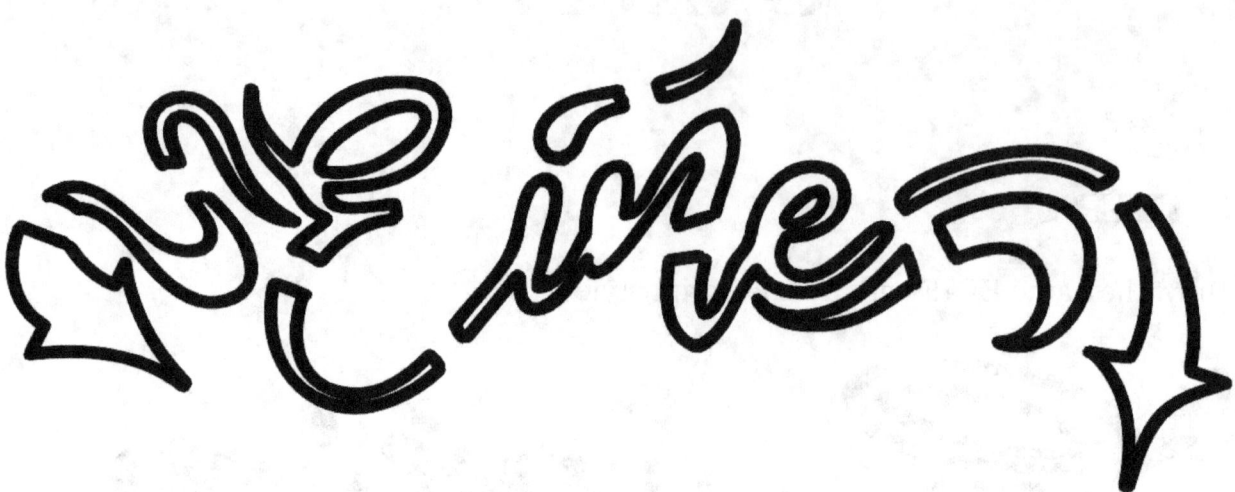

STEP 4

Shade the left and top side edges of the letters giving a 3D effect

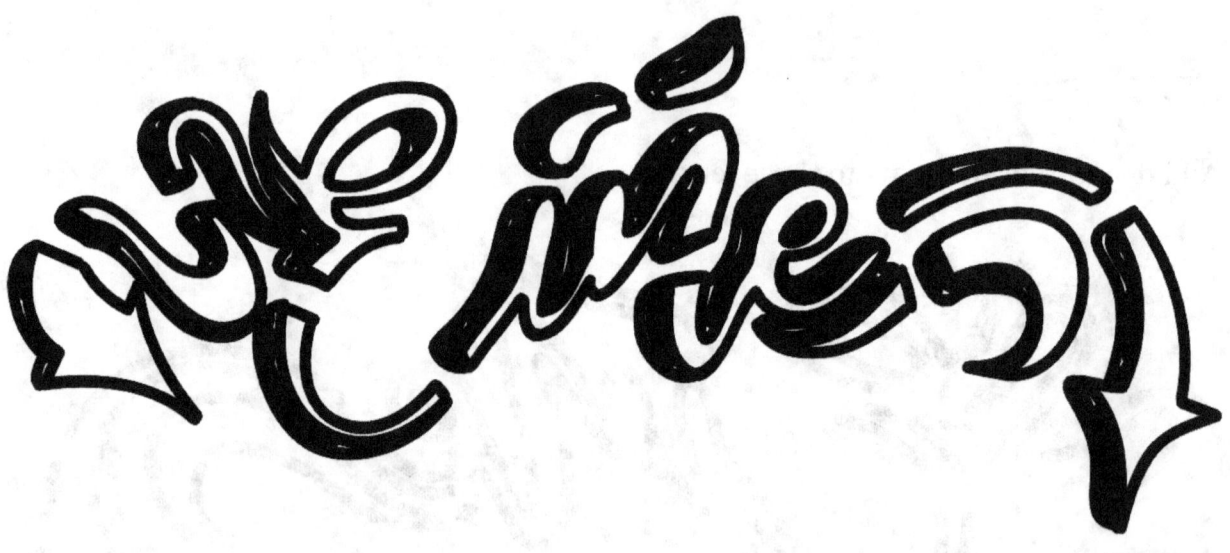

STEP 5

Add crossed lines simulating flashes with a fine stroke

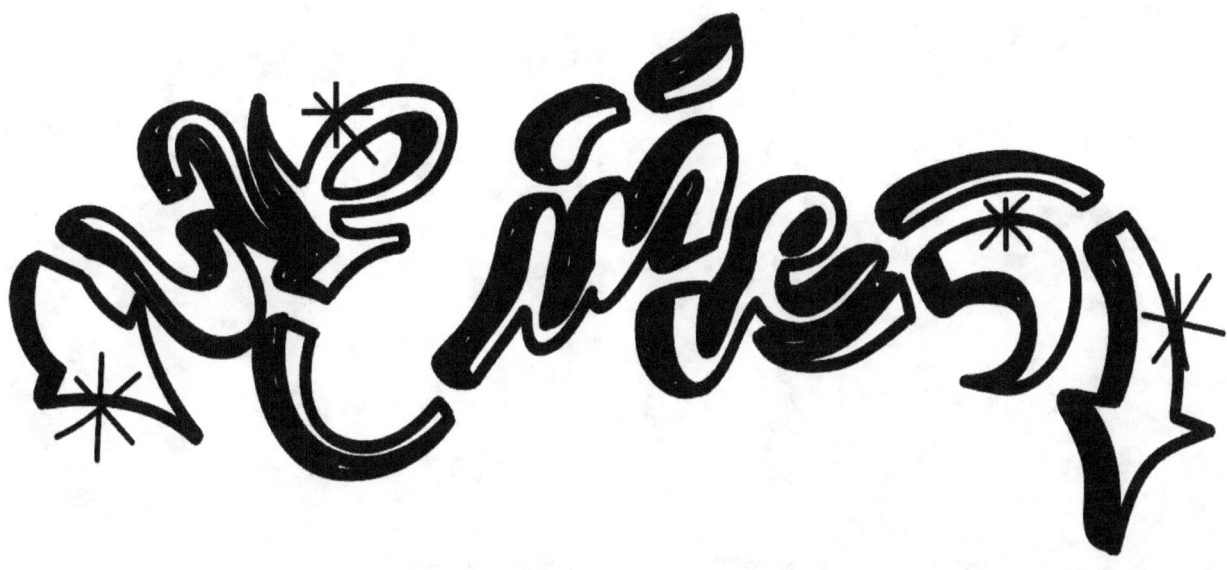

STEP 6

Lastly add an extra detailed brush look surrounding the tag

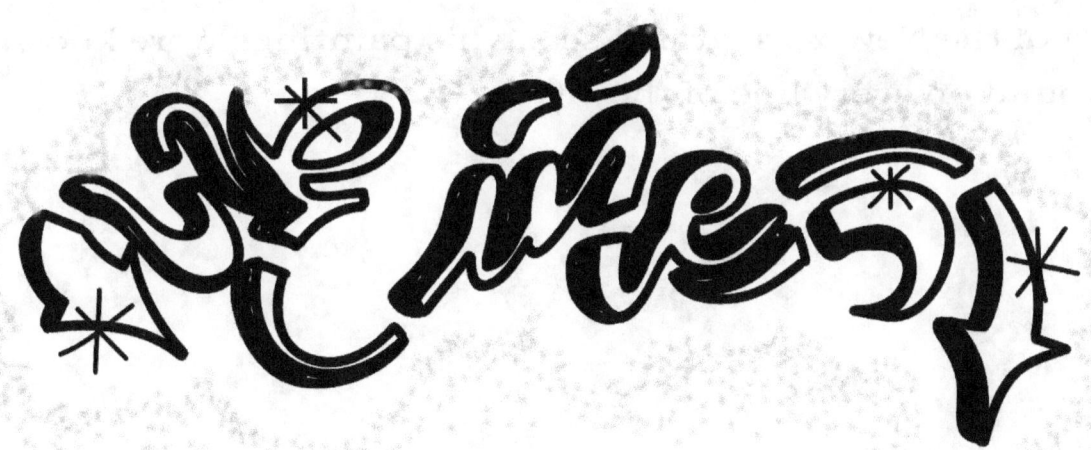

Iz The Wiz:

King of the New York graffti scene his paintings were known to be found on every line of the city

how to DRAW a FREESTYLE GRAFFITI

STEP 1

Draw IZ THE WIZ in simple letters as separated as possible

IZTHEWIZ

STEP 2

Add all the extensions you want by connecting the letters

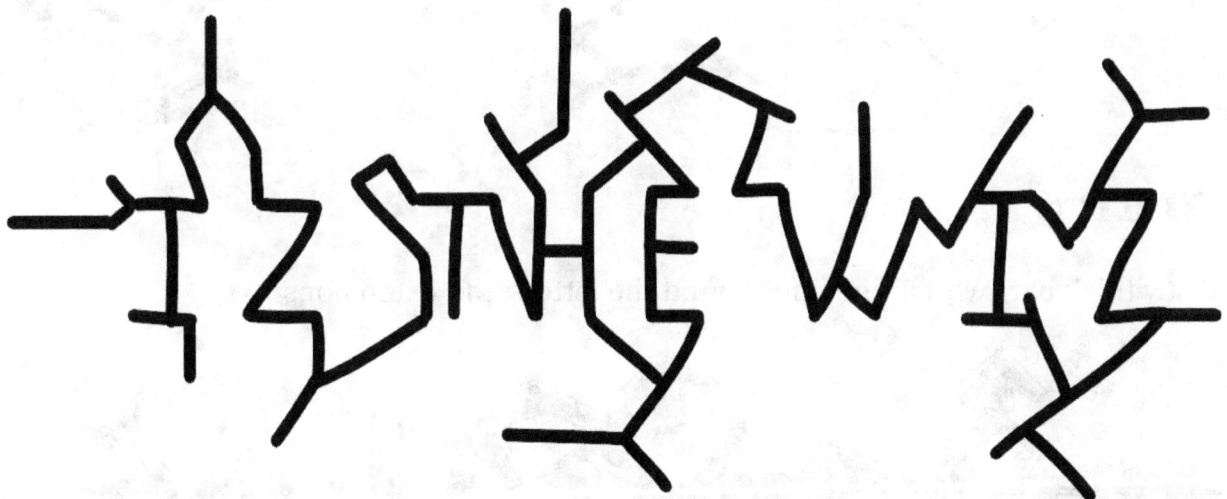

STEP 3

Add arrows to the end of some extensions

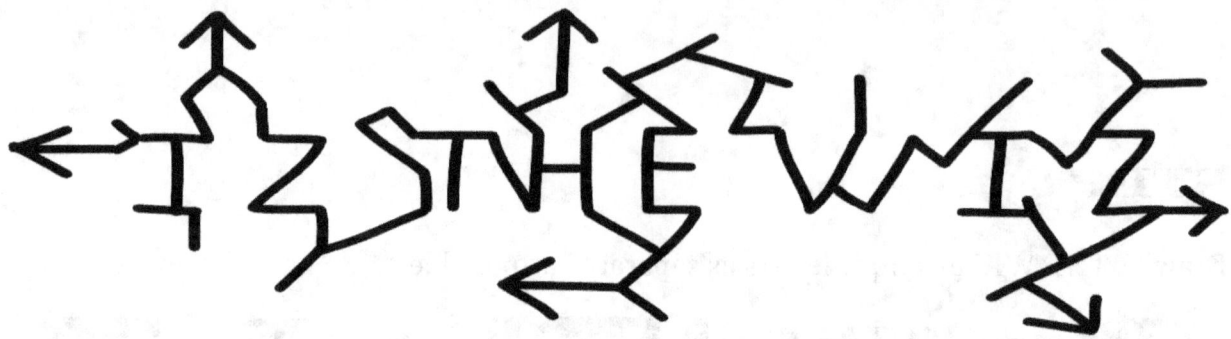

STEP 4

Erase some parts of this sketch

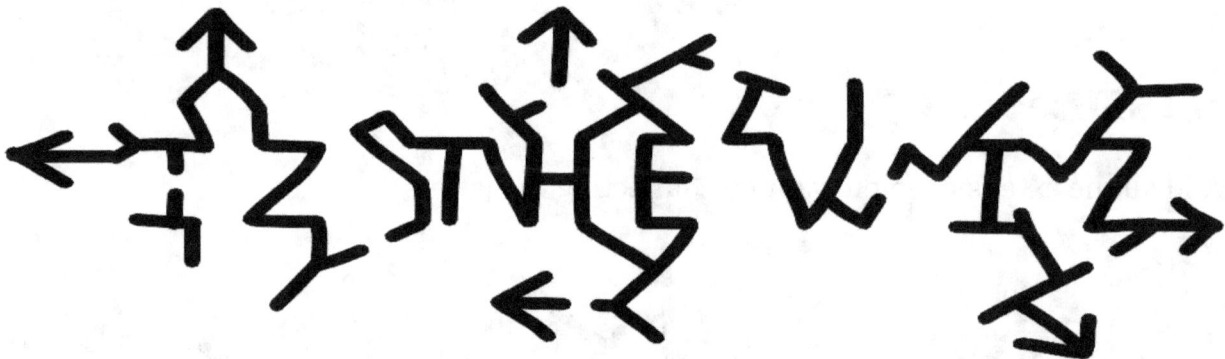

STEP 5

Draw thick bars with a fine line around the letters and extensions

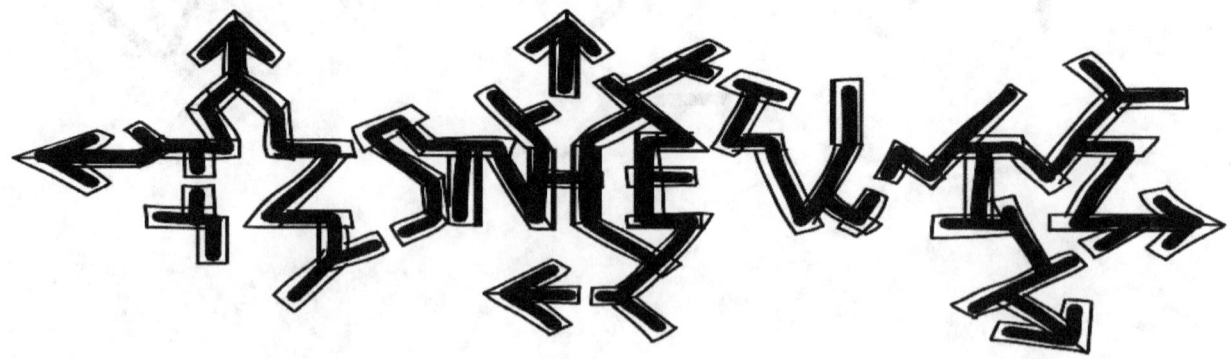

STEP 6

Redo the graffiti following the lines outside and adding intersections between them

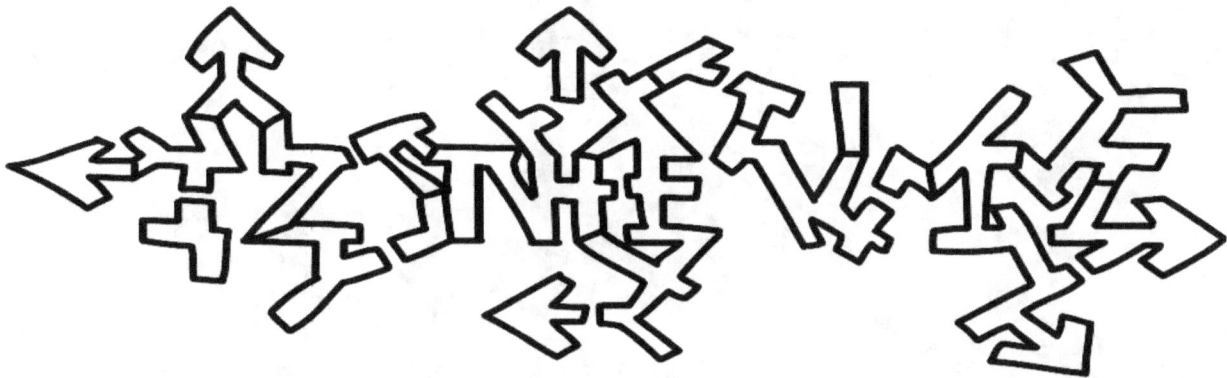

STEP 7

Finally outline and shade in the letters and extensions for a 3D effect. Add bubbles for styling

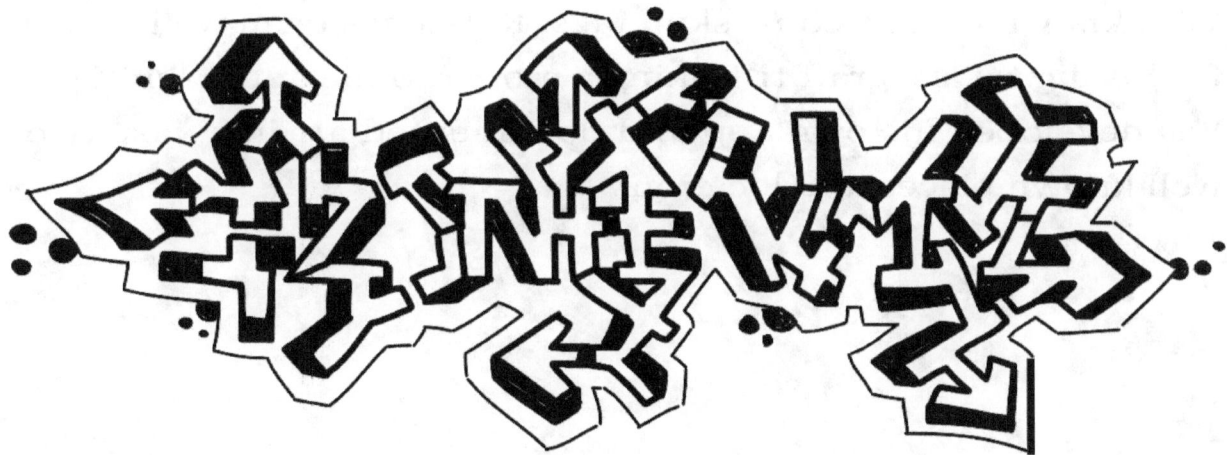

Katsu:

Well known for his iconic skull tags, Katsu has been well known for his digital age graffiti. Taking a more mobile approach Katsu has developed his own app and documented art in a variety of well known places and locations

how to DRAW a FREESTYLE GRAFFITI

STEP 1

Draw the name KATSU with tag style letters

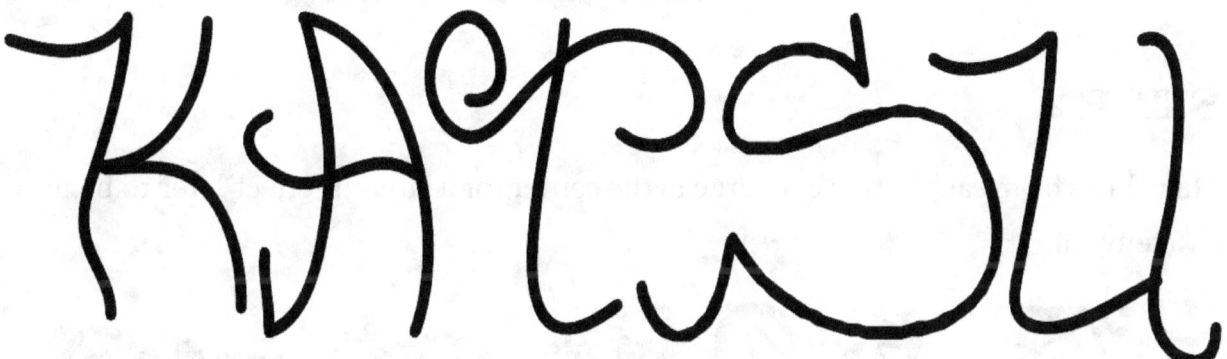

STEP 2

Draw geometric shapes starting from this tag

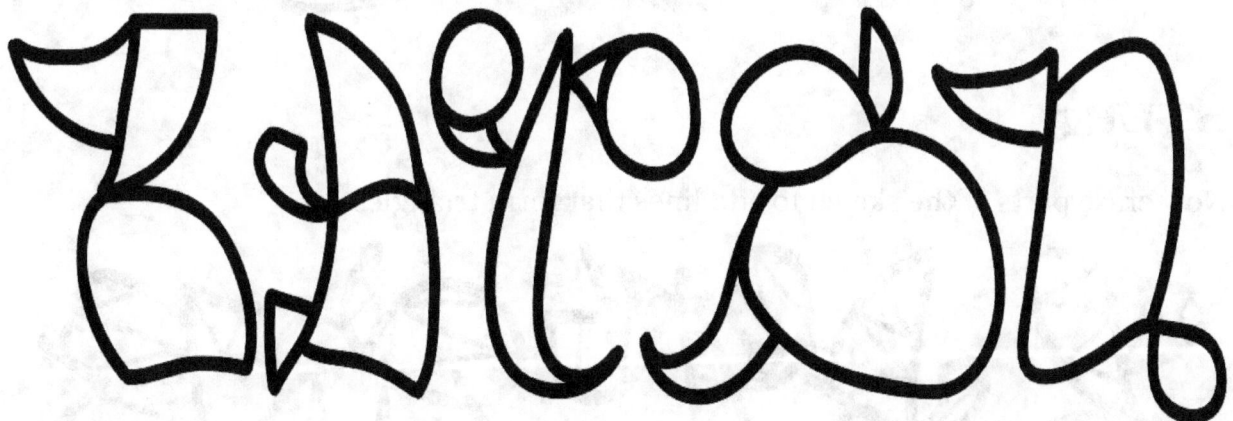

STEP 3

Add lines inside creating triangles in each letter with a fine stroke

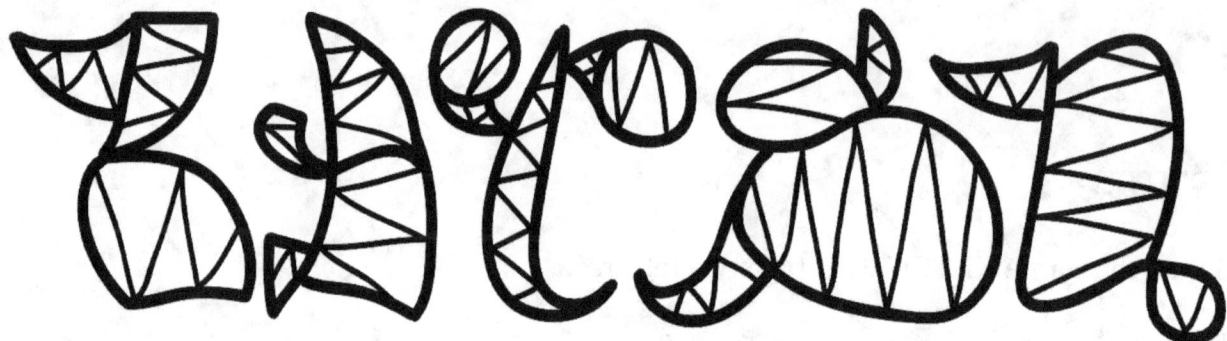

STEP 4

Make lines from each vertex converge in the center for a later 3D effect later to be used as a template

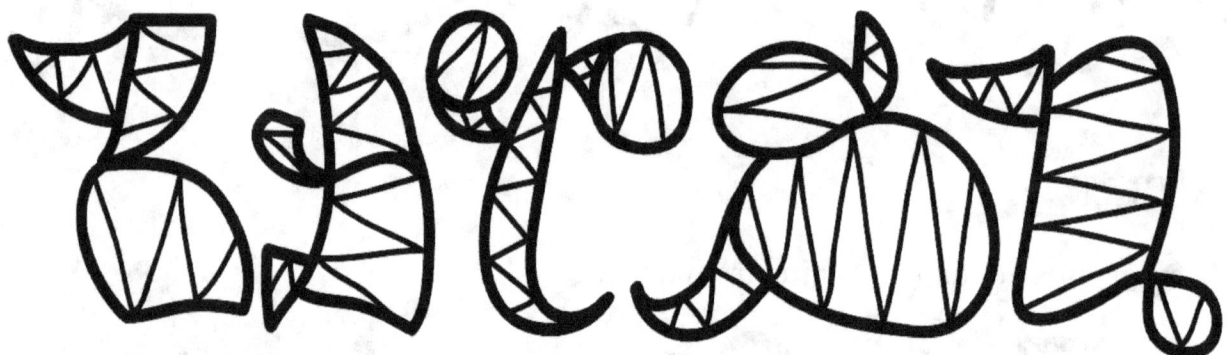

STEP 5

Now erase parts of the sketch to add lines that form triangles

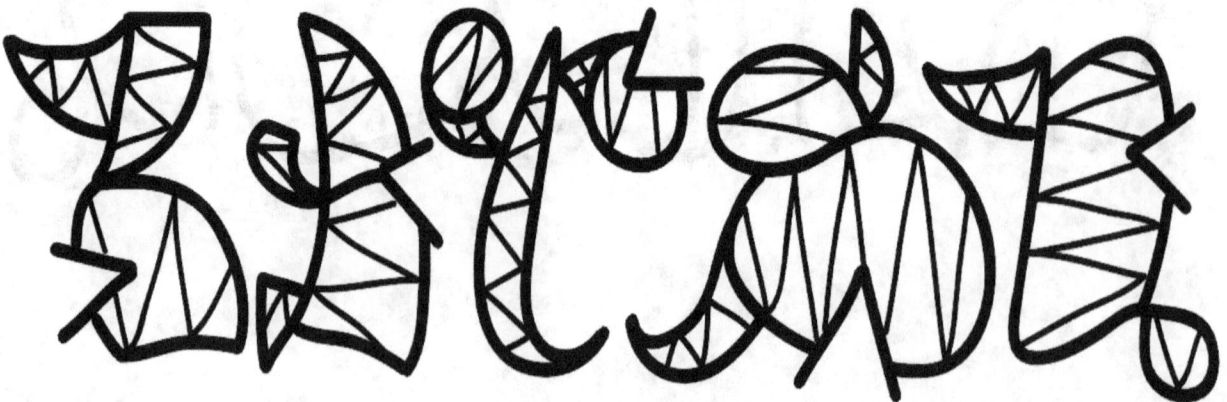

STEP 6

Add a shadow surrounding the letters creating a 3D effect

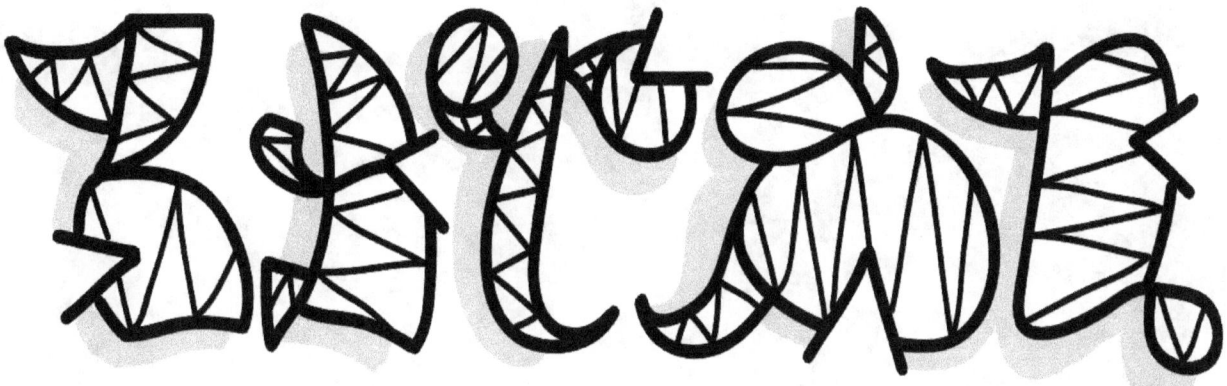

STEP 7

Finally add dashed lines around the letter

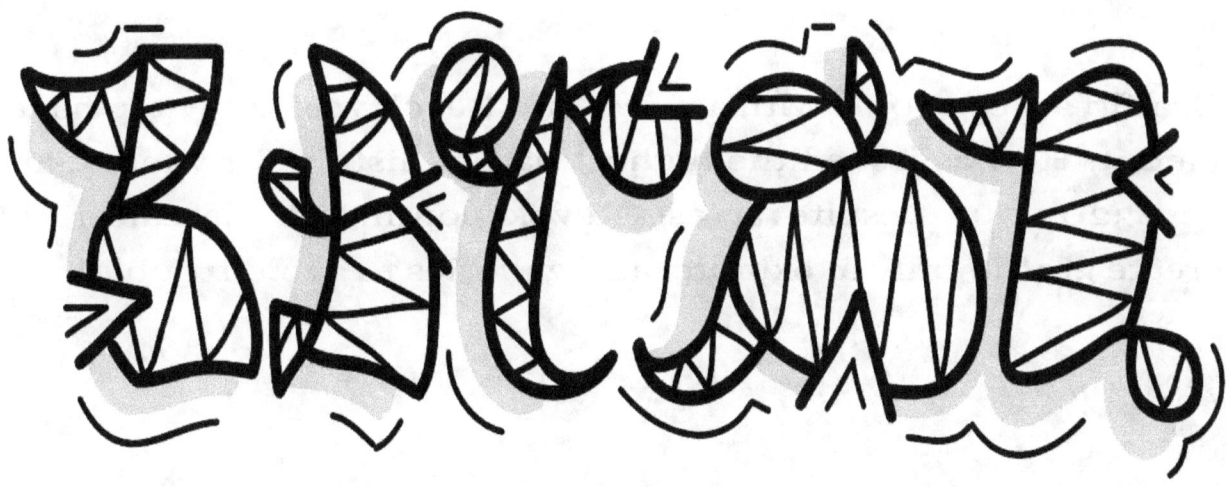

Revok:

Graffiti art can come with a price, and Revok was known to have paid it. He was issued the highest bail in history for vandalism at $320,000. Despite arrest Revok continued thereafter to create graffiti only in exhibits and galleries to avoid trouble

how to DRAW a
FREESTYLE GRAFFITI

STEP 1

Draw the word REVOK with a lower case e

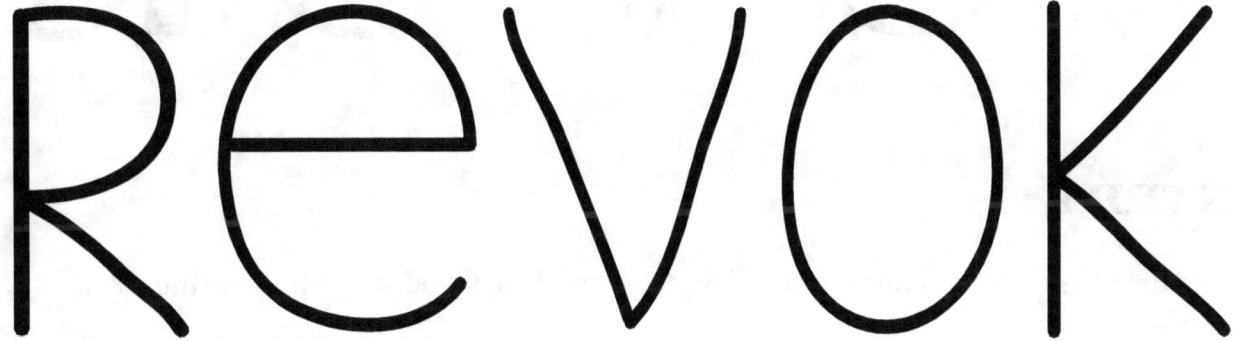

STEP 2

Use these letters as a template to take on geometric form

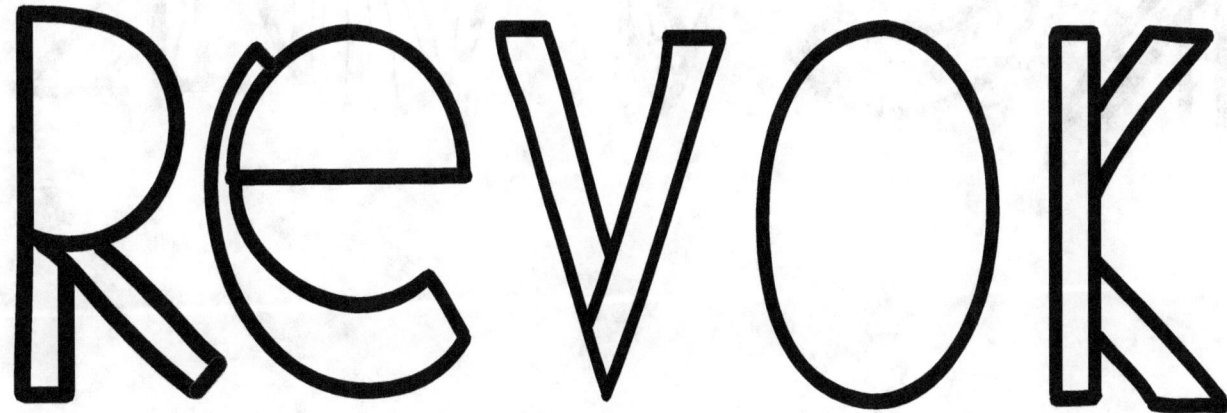

STEP 3

Now add circles as if they were screws where the elements are connected with a fine stroke

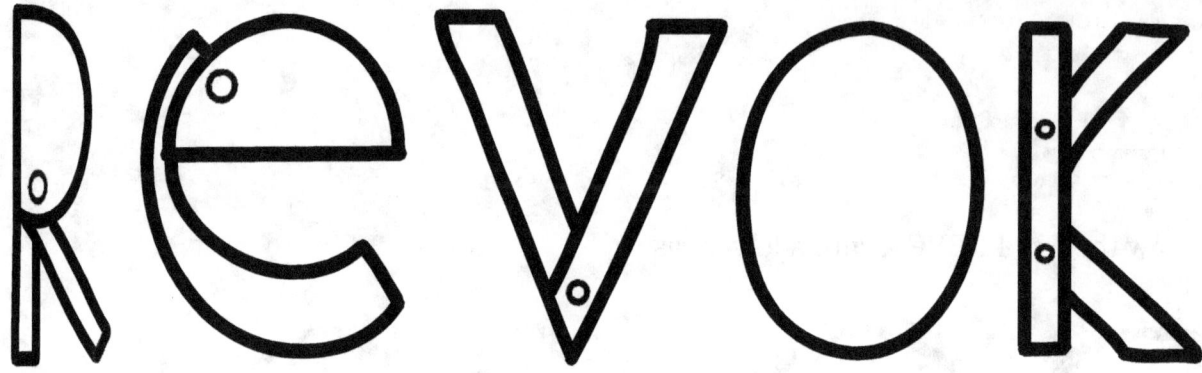

STEP 4

The next step is to add lines in some parts simulating wood with an ultrafine stroke

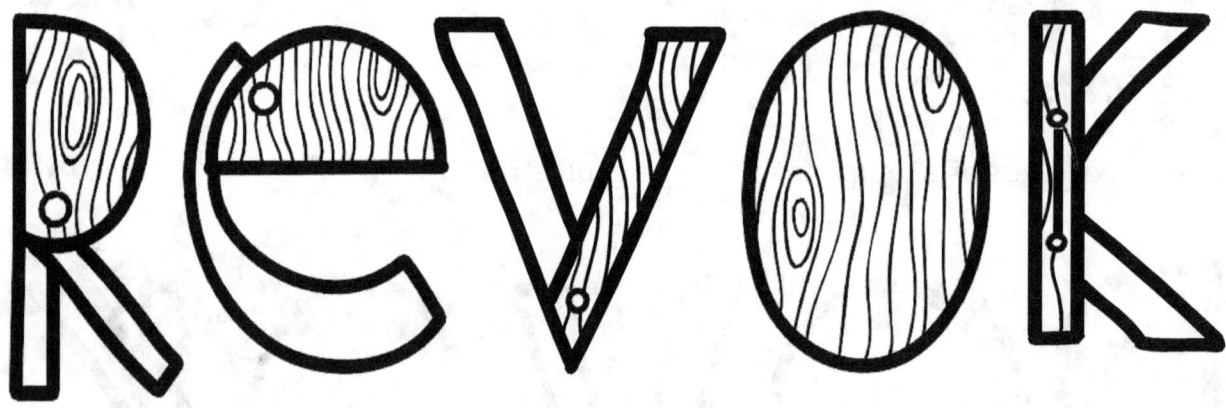

STEP 5

Draw converging shaded long lines down to the center to create a 3D effect

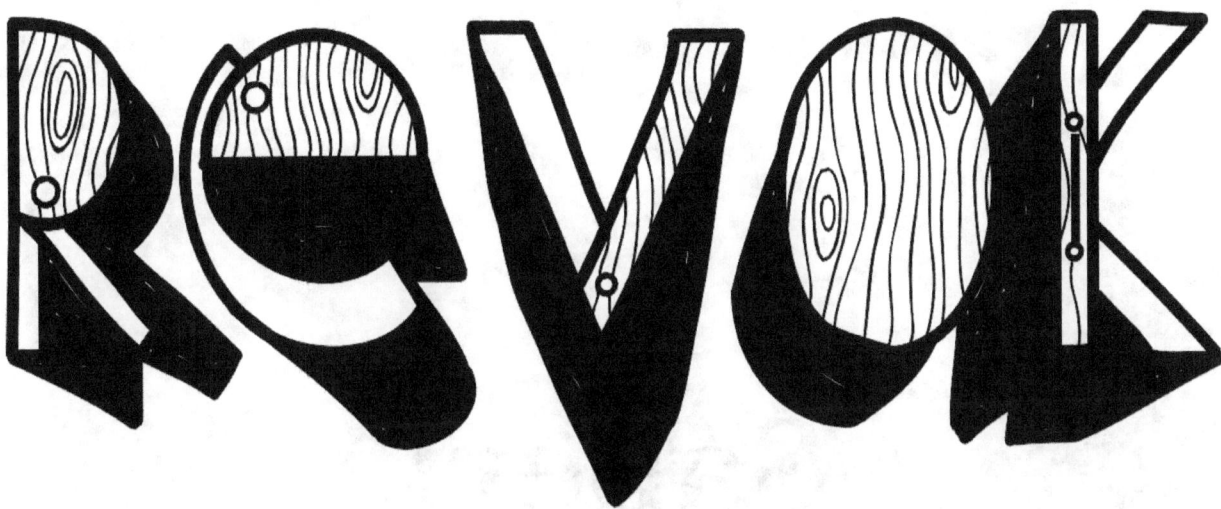

Step 6

Finally add a dashed outline through the sketch with a fine stroke

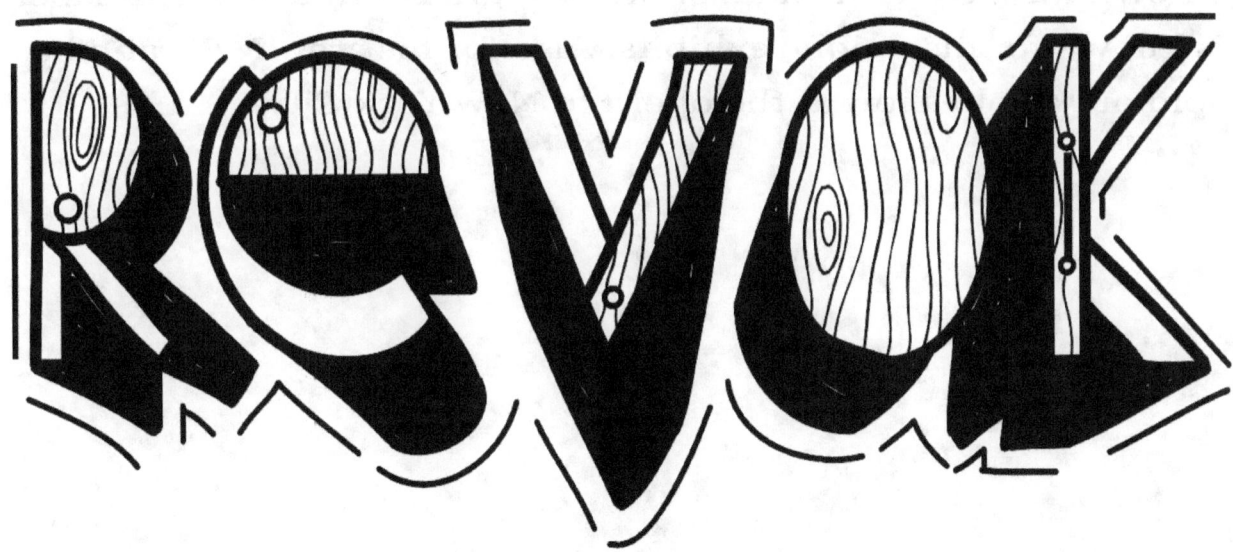

Saber:

Known for having the largest piece of graffiti in the world Saber is known for his unique exhibits. Also for his crew MSK and has sold out a solo show at the opera in New York City

how to DRAW a FREESTYLE GRAFFITI

STEP 1

Draw the name SABER

SABER

STEP 2

Add some serifs and arrows

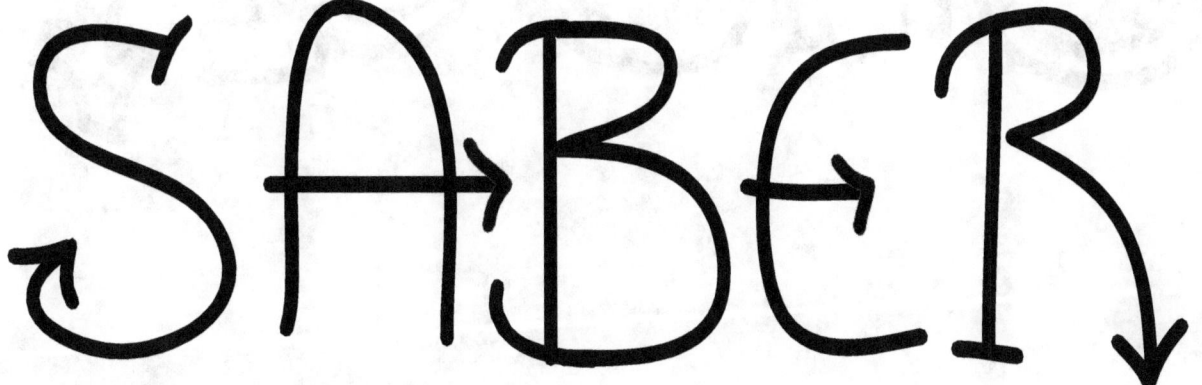

STEP 3

Draw bars around the lines

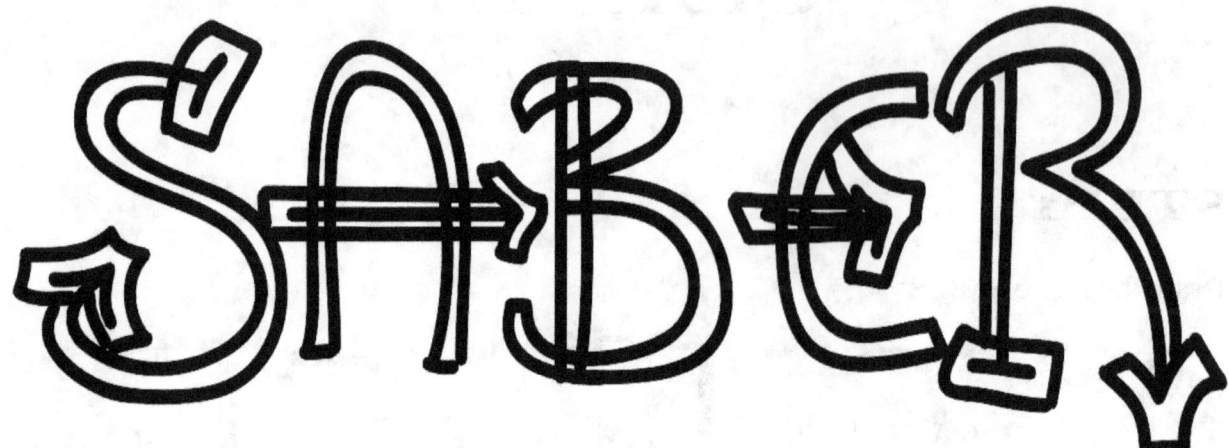

STEP 4

Remove the original letterl lines

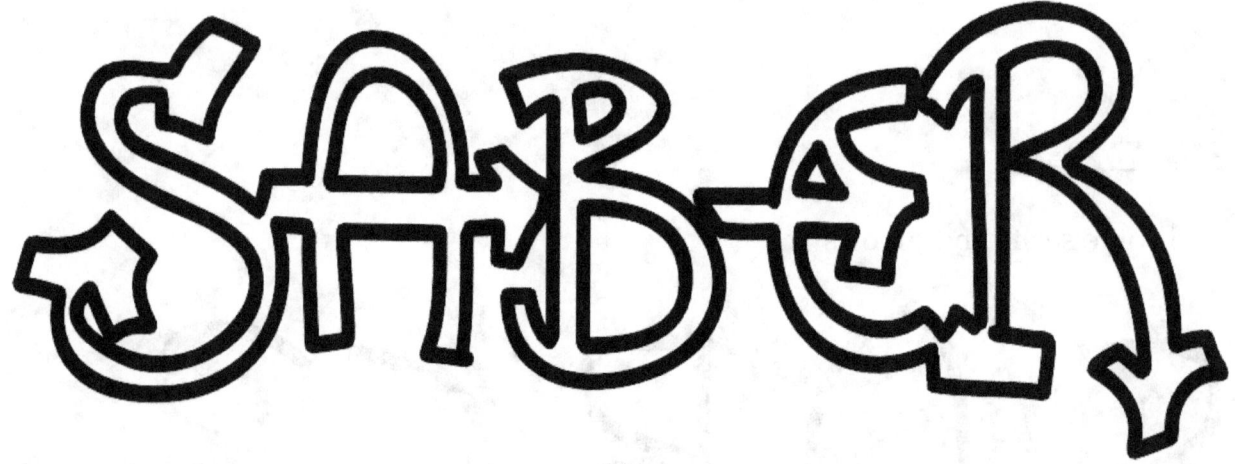

STEP 5

Draw thin vertical lines that will serve as a template

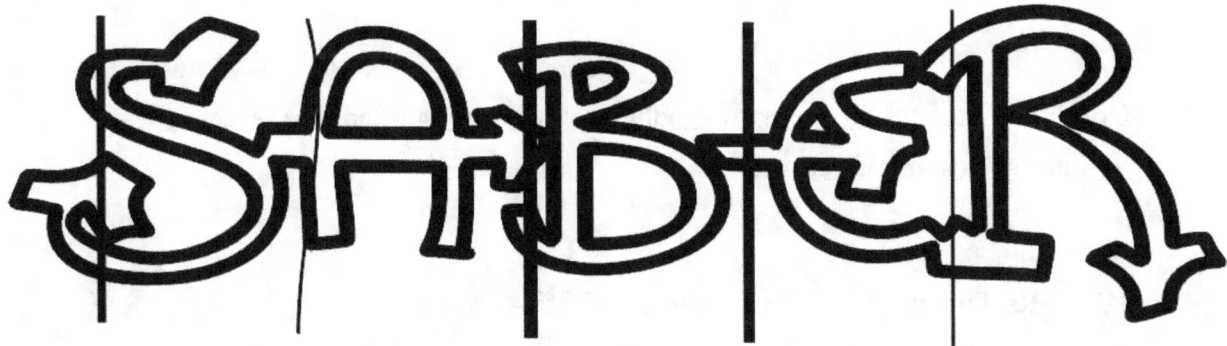

STEP 6

Redraw the sketch from the template lines to your right

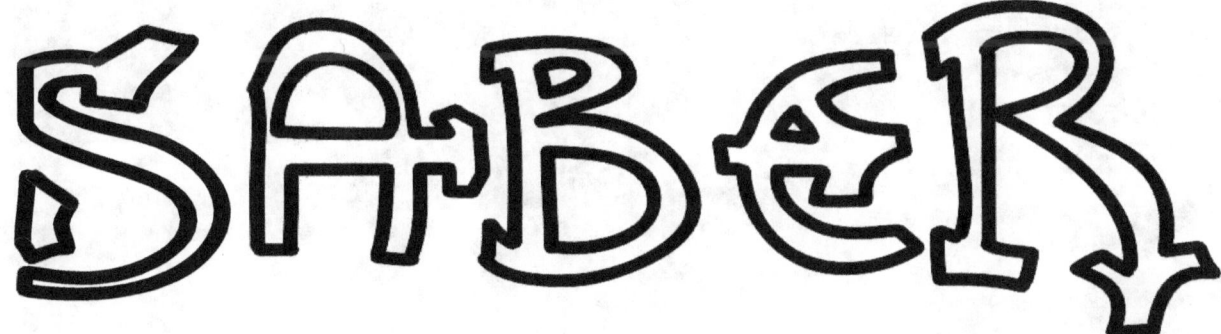

STEP 7

Finally add a very fat outline and a thin line around it

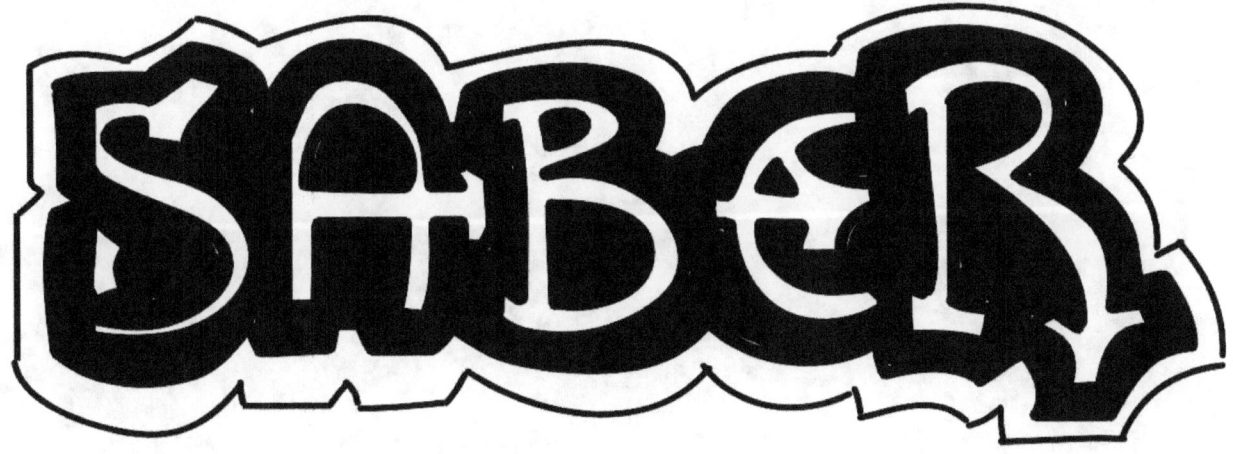

References:

➢ Goodbye Graffiti - https://www.goodbyegraffiti.wa.gov.au/Schools/Teaching-Resources/Glossary-of-Terms

➢ **World's Top 20 Most Famous Graffiti Artists**
https://graffitiknowhow.com/worlds-top-20-most-famous-graffiti-artists/